THE LANGUAGE OF MODERN MUSIC

DONALD MITCHELL

*The Language
of Modern Music*

University of Pennsylvania Press

Philadelphia

To Peter & Mollie du Sautoy

First published in 1963
by Faber and Faber Limited

Revised edition first published 1993
by Faber and Faber Limited.
First published in the United States 1994
by the University of Pennsylvania Press.

Copyright © 1963, 1966, 1976, 1993 by Donald Mitchell
Introduction to 1993 edition copyright © by Edward W. Said

ISBN 0–8122–1543–5

Mitchell, Donald, 1925–
   The language of modern music/by Donald Mitchell;
   with an introduction by Edward Said. — Rev. ed.
      p.   cm.
   Originally published: London: Faber, 1993.
   Includes bibliographical references and index.
   ISBN 0–8122–1543–5
   1. Music—20th century—History and criticism.   I. Title
   ML197.M55   1994
   780′.9′04—dc20

CONTENTS

The artist cannot start from scratch
but he can criticize his forerunners.

E. H. GOMBRICH

NOTE TO REVISED EDITION

Two quotations shall serve in place of a Preface, both of them, I think, relevant to this book. The first is from E. H. Carr's *What is History?* (Pelican Books, 1964, pp. 35–6):

We sometimes speak of the course of history as a 'moving procession'. The metaphor is fair enough, provided it does not tempt the historian to think of himself as an eagle surveying the scene from a lonely crag or as a V.I.P. at the saluting base. Nothing of the kind! The historian is just another dim figure trudging along in another part of the procession. And as the procession winds along, swerving now to the right and now to the left, and sometimes doubling back on itself, the relative positions of different parts of the procession are constantly changing. . . . New vistas, new angles of vision, constantly appear as the procession—and the historian with it—moves along. The historian is part of history. The point in the procession at which he finds himself determines his angle of vision over the past.

The second comes from the American critic Harold Rosenberg's *The Tradition of the New* (London, 1962, p. 23):

What makes any definition of a movement in art dubious is that it never fits the deepest artists in the movement—certainly not as well as, if successful, it does the others. Yet without the definition something essential in those best is bound to be missed. The attempt to define is like a game in which you cannot possibly reach the goal from the starting point but can only close in on it by picking up each time from where the last play landed.

Mr. Rosenberg makes a shrewd point. Nonetheless, nothing that has been written about the first edition of this book makes me regret my attempt to play the game. I have taken the opportunity that this third edition affords to add a new chapter, 'Music or "Music"?', which first appeared in *The Times Literary Supplement* (issue of January 4th, 1968).

London, 1969   D.M.

PREFACE TO NEW EDITION (1993)

After a performance at Aldeburgh of one of his works from the early forties—a very rarely performed work at the time (it was the *Scottish Ballad*, for two pianos and orchestra)—I remember Britten remarking to me that, for him, encountering the piece again was like looking 'at a very old photograph'. There was a strong implication of time past and fading round the edges; and I must confess that somewhat similar feelings have been aroused in me whenever I have turned over a few pages of this book, most of it written—I find it hard to believe—in 1963. Thirty years ago! Not yet a match for Alan Bennett, but it soon will be.

And the book must have had readers, otherwise why all the reprints and revisions of revisions? Moreover, not only readers of the English text but of the various translations that have been made. Could there be a list more eccentric than this? Japanese, Greek, Serbo-Croat, Spanish; and a translation into Russian made by a gifted postgraduate student in Moscow who needed it for her thesis. Its later publication was planned but the turmoil of *perestroika* dashed it. I wonder what conclusions might be drawn from that small tower of Babel?

My spelling out details of the publication, as concisely as possible, may be helpful because in fact they represent not so much internal modifications of the óriginal text—there have been remarkably few of those—as additions, in the shape of new chapters.

The first edition, published in 1963, comprised the first three chapters, plus an unnumbered Postscript. The book's original design—typography, brass and jacket—was the work of the legendary Berthold Wolpe. We have retained the Bodoni typeface but the cover, naturally enough, reflects the Faber profile of the nineties. The 'language' of the book's design may have changed a bit but I'd like to pay tribute to Berthold's brilliant skills, which brought a terrific style to the book on its launching.

In 1966 there was a new edition and the first of the additions: the Postscript (1963) was allotted a chapter number, and there fol-

Preface to New Edition (1993)

lowed two further chapters, V and VI, the last being a Postlude (1965). There was then another new edition in 1968, on which occasion a new last chapter, 'Music or "Music"?', was added. Nothing, I think, was changed in the reprints of 1976 (but Picasso's portrait of Stravinsky and Schiele's of Schoenberg now graced the back cover of this first paperback edition) and 1983; which brings us to 1993, and not—luckily—to any more additions or extensions from me: what, in any case, having used up 'Postscript' and 'Postlude', might any new addition have been called? We have now something we have not had before, a Prelude, in the shape of an altogether fascinating introduction by Edward Said, much more rewarding than anything I might have dreamed up, although surely too generous in his assessment of my old text—and too kind to Strauss! To my mind, he hits a fundamental nail right on the head, early on in his essay: 'Modernity is in fact made, not given, and great artists (and great critics) give that creation a recognizable profile, one that is never static, but always a constantly negotiated relationship with the past, as well as the present.'

That, it seems to me, cannot be said too often, though it's rarely said as elegantly and concisely as by Professor Said (why, I begin to wonder, didn't *he* write this book?). It would certainly have earned the passionate agreement of Britten, had he had a chance to read Professor Said's introduction. As we know, he showed no conspicuous enthusiasm for reading books about music, which made it all the more surprising when he told me, long, long after this book had been published, that he had read it not once but *twice*. If that was true, and I have no reason to doubt it, then it must surely be the only book by a music critic that was thus singled out by the composer. Not for polite praise, either, let me hasten to add. He made only two comments, both of them interesting. First, that even after the second time round, he found it inconceivable that anyone could suggest or argue that tonality could ever be replaced by any other 'system', so fundamental was it to his own creativity. He just didn't understand how the argument could even be put. If one was talking about the 'language' of music, then for him tonality *was* that language. Secondly, however, he 'loved' (his word) the last chapters and their scepticism about the new 'music', which just about matched his own.

I'm sometimes asked—and sometimes ask myself—if I have any 'regrets' about the book, i.e., does it trouble me that the idea of a unifying language, common as it was among the fine and applied arts at different stages during the period I was writing about, did not prevail? Not at all. It was how it looked at the time the book was written; and indeed, if I am forced to place a value on it, then it seems to me to reside in the immediacy of much of my text, in its reflection, albeit an imperfect and individual one, of what it was like to be thinking and writing about music in the late fifties and early sixties. Hence not only the impossibility but undesirability of revising the text. History itself has done that for me.

In some ways, moreover, the idea *did* prevail, though not perhaps quite as Schoenberg had imagined it would. There is scarcely a composer whose techniques have not been significantly affected by his thinking. Even someone like Britten, in whose music, especially in his last years, twelve-note propositions took on an increasing significance and complexity. Here I certainly do have a regret, that he is no longer around for a discussion—or at any rate an attempted discussion—of the new paths he was exploring in his late works and which received, I realize in retrospect, cursory treatment in the text that he read. Cursory too, and much more serious in its inadequacy, was the scant attention—no more than lip-service—I paid Debussy, perhaps the one feature of my text I feel really guilty about today. However, I am now, I hope, less ignorant than I was, and shall continue to try to make amends elsewhere. I was sorely tempted to include in this new edition a long study, entitled 'Cradles of the New: Paris and Vienna at the turn of the century', a contribution I made to the Tokyo Summer Festival in 1986, and which, I believe, does something more like justice to Debussy's innovating genius. But this would have been to embark on what I wanted to resist, the process of further revision and—in this case—the complicating factor of expiation. I have settled for living with my guilt, at least within the covers of this book.

Finally, to return to Britten (himself a great admirer of Debussy), I am sorry not to be able to congratulate him on the rightness of his convictions and his instinct. Because on the whole, in whatever highly modified or qualified form, tonality, as we move into the twenty-first century, seems likely not just to be with us but still to play a vigorous and fertilizing role in the many languages in which music will speak to us.

London, December 1992   Donald Mitchell

INTRODUCTION by *Edward W. Said*

The title, as well as a great deal of the body of this extraordinary book, makes the point that modern music has, or perhaps at bottom is, a language. To a casual reader this may seem plausible enough, but not only is it an uncommon view, it has not before been urged with such brilliance and insight. Donald Mitchell's watchwords are *communication, comprehensibility, speech, address, understanding,* and their cognates. These anchor the rigorous critical intelligence at work in this book, as well as an attitude to music (and other things as well) implacably opposed to obfuscation, hermeticism, provinciality, jargon, and *their* cognates. Thus, although *The Language of Music* is the work of a fully professional, thoroughly schooled and practised musicologist, it is most certainly not intended as a tract only for other accredited musicologists or a band of trained insiders; on the contrary, even though it has quite a lot to say to them, it is above all a book about how modern music acquired and therefore has a language, and how this music is a full partner in the enterprise of Western cultural modernism.

There is an affecting directness, even simplicity, to this argument that rather belies its enormous sophistication and rhetorical skill. For modernity is not simply *now*, any more than history is (as American parlance often has it) what is over and done with. In America, 'you're history' is like telling people that their fate is the memory hole; in the context of this book, history is what must be grasped, understood, constituted. Using two shrewdly chosen epigraphs from E.H. Carr and Harold Rosenberg, Mitchell accepts, on the one hand, the historian's role as being in history, moving, writing, judging along with it, playing the part of an actor whose words express 'new angles of vision'. On the other hand, he realizes simultaneously that no definitions can totally represent the work of the best artists in a movement, even though without these definitions still more things would be missed. Modernity is in fact made, not given, and great artists (and great critics) give that creation a recognizable profile, one that is never static, but always itself a constantly negotiated relationship with the past, as well as the present. 'The artist cannot start from scratch but he can criticize his forerunner,' says E.H. Gombrich in a sentence that further clarifies Mitchell's view of modernity as a critical—that is, an alert, reasoned, often contentious—engagement with the past.

Out of this debate comes European modernism which, as Mitchell painstakingly shows, took shape on a wide front, with music, literature, painting, sculpture, design contributing different, although related, elements. Yet, he quite correctly points out that the modernist arts do not lurch forward all together, in synchrony and according to an orderly schedule:

> . . . the timescales upon which music and visual arts operate are not identical. Painting, as it were, lives through its history, its innovations, its styles, even more swiftly than does music. There may be very good reasons why the eye is able to assimilate new modes of expression more quickly and easily than the ear . . . Perspective could be renounced, a new visual language organized, and eventually relinquished, all within the space of a few years. Music, however, was slower to cut itself free from tonality, and slower still to build up a new means of order; which is suggestive of the relative slowness with which basic innovations in music evolve (p. 89).

Mitchell's largest, and most exciting claim, is that Arnold Schoenberg—in many ways the hero of *The Language of Modern Music*—and Igor Stravinsky bring to light 'new realms of feeling' in their art, not simply by emoting or displaying themselves, but (and this is crucial) by a rigorous application of technique, formal construction, sustained discipline *within* their art.

This last point is where the catch is, I think. It is relatively easy to speak, say, of literary innovations and of new vocabularies to a general audience: T.S. Eliot's technical experiments in the broken, quotation-filled lines of *The Wasteland*, for example, are readily evident, especially since the lines from older writers like Baudelaire and Dante that Eliot subpoenas for use are quoted respectfully, or at least with affection. There is a good deal of nostalgia in Joyce's use of Homer in *Ulysses*. But Schoenberg's wholesale rejection of the tonal system is, as Mitchell puts it, much more extreme and unsentimental, an act of total abjuring, a rejection of what is 'natural' to our ears. We experience it as violent; Schoenberg's earliest audiences were just as violently opposed to it. 'Not music' and 'not worth listening to' was the commonest form of rejection, with results in ignorance, resentment, even anger that prevented performances until well into the 1930s and 1940s. Despite this, Mitchell avers, Schoenberg's method overcame its opponents and established a new vocabulary—derived from the dodecaphonic row—for music, precisely because the achievement genuinely summed up, then went beyond the huge musical achievement of nineteenth-century Germany as it culminated in Wagnerian chromaticism and tonal instability.

This is paradoxical: Schoenberg would have been unable to re-create 'a language for music in the twentieth century had he *not* been born out of the great tradition which he had to abandon'. Mitchell analyses not only Schoenberg's assumption, as it were, of traditional tonal music but his abandonment of it, both of which together make possible the achievement of a new language. Moreover, and more impressively, Mitchell helps us to appreciate the full gravity of that abandonment by way of the psychological resistances to it bred, like unconscious fears, in audiences who quite naturally are dependent on habit and what Conrad in *Heart of Darkness* called the world of straightforward facts. Thus the awesome, backbreaking job of working through tonality, the resistance to modernism, and the intricacies of a new method for composing music are the constituents of Schoenberg's claim to innovation, and the triumph of a truly modern language that Mitchell so skillfully presents for our considered attention here.

Although he does not mention it, there is one work of musico-philosophical analysis that resembles *The Language of Modern Music* and yet differs from it most interestingly: Theodor Adorno's *The Philosophy of Modern Music*, as it is called in its only English translation (the original German refers specifically not to modern but to 'new' music). First published in 1948 Adorno's masterpiece emerges from out of the ruins of the Hegelian tradition, recording in it the heroic, almost suicidal efforts of Schoenberg—Adorno's teacher—to develop 'new' music out of such important antecedents as Beethoven's late style, the divagations of German Romanticism, Wagner, and the triumph of capitalism. Like Georg Lukacs's *History and Class Consciousness*, *The Philosophy of Modern Music* explores the philosophic antinomies, those irreconcilable opposites, inherent to modern society (for example in the relationship between subject and object), arguing more forcefully than anyone before Adorno that music and the contemporary social order could not be reconciled, and that Schoenberg's intransigence, his forbiddingly self-enforced regimen, his inhuman method, signified nothing less than that music has accepted its fate, 'at the very border of insanity', to remain in an 'aporia' from which there was no exit. The peculiarity, not to say repulsiveness of such music (which Adorno admires unreservedly), is that it can be neither heard properly, nor in the end paid much attention to, precisely because it is meant to be a symbol of modern society's own degradation:

> Modern music sacrifices itself to this effort. It has taken upon itself all the darkness and guilt of the world. Its fortune lies in the perception of misfortune; all of its beauty is in denying itself the illusion of beauty. No one wishes to become involved with art—individuals as little as collectives. It dies away unheard, without even an echo. If time crystallizes around that music which has been heard, revealing its radiant quintessence, music which has not been heard falls into empty time like an impotent bullet. Modern music spontaneously aims towards this last experience, evidenced hourly in mechanical music. Modern music sees absolute oblivion as its goal. It is the surviving message of despair from the shipwrecked.[1]

Apocalyptic and highly wrought (some would say 'overwrought'), this passage immediately contrasts with Mitchell's, I think, more realistic and humane view of what in effect is the same phenomenon.

Leaving aside the enormous difference in tone between Adorno's darkly brooding metaphysical rebarbativeness and Mitchell's energetic and informally engaging discourse, there are three radical distinctions to be noted between these two major statements. One, of course, is that Mitchell correctly assumes that Schoenberg's music is if not enjoyable in the conventional sense, then at least pleasurable, listenable to, and that it will survive, indeed more than survive, by changing the norms for listening to and composing in the whole field of modern music. Perhaps the difference also

---

[1] Theodor W. Adorno: *Philosophy of Modern Music*, trans. Anne G. Mitchell and Wesley V. Blomster, New York, Seabury Press, 1973, p. 133.

reflects the divergence in historical generation between Adorno and Mitchell, to say nothing of the difference in philosophical traditions, the one metaphysical and dialectical, the other more empirical, open, and optimistic.

Second, Adorno's view of modern music is that only Schoenberg produced it, Stravinsky and Bartók effectively remaining on the sidelines, the former a proto-fascistic sleight-of-hand artist, the latter a folklorist and minor populist. Adorno's Schoenberg is drawn both as an Old Testament prophet and a kind of monopolist, whose interest in totality, rigor, and renunciation allowed him not only to absorb the whole of the tradition, but also to exclude everyone else in the process of renouncing it. Mitchell's is a more attractive portrait. Although there is no scanting of the man's crusty, stubborn persistence in working things out his way, no matter the cost, the Viennese composer who stands forth in Mitchell's prose is a human being that listeners, other composers, as well as other artists, would recognize as someone interested, like all of them, in actually using his art to communicate.

Third, Mitchell supposes that to understand Schoenberg one must also understand and appreciate Stravinsky, the other, the twin great figure who forged the language of modern music. Adorno is quite unyielding about allowing any such importance to be accorded the Russian. 'Stravinsky's sweetest composer's dream,' he says bitingly, 'is versatile submissiveness and hysterical obedience—the very pattern of the authoritarian character which is today in formulation on all sides.'[2]

In a passage of extraordinarily attractive clarity Mitchell connects Stravinsky with Schoenberg as follows:

> Despite the wealth of new fertile ground explored in each case, both composers had, in a sense, to begin afresh; Schoenberg to grow into the Method, Stravinsky to evolve a relation with the past. Thus side by side the two main streams of the New in music developed. (p. 96)

Later, Mitchell elucidates with regard to Stravinsky by saying that if Schoenberg's twelve-note method was a language, then Stravinsky's neo-classicism was a style whose achievement was to tie him not to the immediate, but to the distant past. Unlike his

---

[2] Adorno, *op. cit.*, pp. 200–1.

predecessors who responded to their immediate ancestors, musically speaking, Stravinsky's traversal of time into the distant past was a gesture undertaken (again paradoxically) to assert his own traditionlessness, and then also to make the past the subject or theme of his music. I quote Mitchell once more: 'The "new" part of the (musical) world that Stravinsky has made accessible to active creative feeling is no less than the past itself' (p. 101–2). We therefore find the two distinguished musical creators of the twentieth century exposing new areas of human experience to the musical impulse, thereby enabling a language with altogether greater scope and deeper reach for the purposes of communication by musical means.

Mitchell is, in the main, right to see in the two not only the beginning but also the end of the musical period, that of modernism itself, which he sees as being succeeded by a series of rather less interesting styles. Sometimes he refers to this as 'music' (the inverted commas delimiting an effigy rather than the real thing) or non-music, perhaps the 'noise' to which in an uncompelling and ephemeral work Jacques Attali has given too much, albeit fussily affected, attention.[3] In a comparable gesture Adorno writes an autumnal essay whose subject is 'new music growing old', music that has lost the force of original creation and has become formulaic, inauthentic, epigonal. Yet if I were to venture the smallest disagreement with Mitchell's scheme, I would say that for all its superb force it is, for me at least, like Adorno's in this respect: a little too tight, perhaps even deterministic, not quite flexible enough to admit powerful alternatives that stand outside the mainstream it so intelligently abumbrates.

Take the case of Richard Strauss, rather brusquely dismissed after *Elektra* (1909) by Mitchell as a composer of little interest. Glenn Gould has advanced the (admittedly exaggerated) claim that Strauss is *the* greatest figure of twentieth-century music; according to Gould, in his entirely inwardly directed musical career Strauss is a model of 'harmonic infallibility' as well as an astonishing instance of vast technical competence. Since Gould is also a Schoenbergian, the claim for Strauss is by no means a narrow one, since in him Gould also sees a trajectory of such interest as to scandalize any

---

[3] *Noise: The Political Economy of Music*, Minneapolis, University of Minnesota Press, 1985.

developmental schemes like Adorno's or Mitchell's. I am inclined to agree with this view of Strauss, whose late works need to be heard neither as a simple rejection of neo-classicism or twelve-note method, nor as an atavistic regression to an earlier, simpler time, but as a contrapuntal alternative to them. Far from standing for obliviousness or cowardice, the Oboe Concerto or *Metamorphosen*, and even *Capriccio*, are more complex works when heard together with the Webern *Variations*, for instance, or *The Rake's Progress*, brilliantly resourceful alternatives to Webern's or Stravinsky's re-investigations of eighteenth-century forms, reinvesting them with tonality and a certain, often corrosive irony.

My feeling is that Mitchell's just admiration for modernism unnecessarily commits him to a melioristic, and slightly exclusivist scheme which imposes rejections and dismissals that are not at all necessary. Consider the post-*Elektra* Strauss as having deliberately fashioned an independent re-embrace of tonality, with often remarkable success (especially when his librettist was von Hofmannsthal). And Mitchell's own *aperçu*—on the informative role played in musical modernism by literary texts—can be applied to Strauss's unparalleled inventiveness in *his* use of first-rate texts. I would then go on to say that after Wagner and Debussy, with tonality threatened or at least revised, everyone who composed, including Strauss, was in effect using harmonic schemes and idioms as a second nature, not innocently or without ideological thrust. One can listen to Strauss therefore as a third revision of the tonal system, Wagner's being the first, Schoenberg's the second.

Part of the problem is Mitchell's worry that undue attention to neo-Romantics like Strauss might distract from or somehow diminish the modernity of modernism's innovatory message. He puts this as follows: 'our present historical situation is confusing because we live in a period of transition, when our emotional entanglement with the past tends to corrupt our insight' (p. 73). This stricture against 'emotional entanglement with the past' is unduly harsh, and goes a little against the generosity of Mitchell's writing. By itself, modernity is no guarantee of good music, any more than 'the past' is *ipso facto* a bad thing for modern music. Part of what Mitchell himself hears in Schoenberg and Stravinsky is what has been nourished in them by the past. Besides no one more than Mitchell knows that in great modernist artists like Proust, whose formal novelistic techniques are so revolutionary, the past, memory, recollection are the very core of his achievement.

My point here is not really to challenge the main lines of Mitchell's argument, but to release it from its own confinements and open it out in ways that strike me as really quite compatible with his own interpretative predilections. Music in the twentieth century (I speak here of music, not 'music' in Mitchell's devastatingly accurate encapsulation of mediocre music) is change and exploration. Even in the later Schoenberg and Stravinsky, those two Titans of modernism, one can, however, detect some hardening of the arteries, some relentlessness, some doctrinaire, even uninspired composing. Certainly don't throw out the baby with the bath water, but must we cherish every sud and every bubble? The forward-looking enthusiasm for modernity that carries Mitchell so compellingly through the occasional aridities of Henze, for instance, or the altogether minor accomplishments of a Joseph Haas or Gerald Finzi, requires us, his re-readers in 1992, to use his tonic writing in order to take up again the case of composers like Strauss, Boulez, Messiaen, perhaps even Stockhausen—and also, Berio, Weill, Busoni, Carter, Ives, Cage, Bolcom, plus many, many others—whose achievements and reputations are still in flux, still in need of reassessment, above all of re-listening.

Yet it is precisely because Donald Mitchell has so finely presented us not just with a survey, but with a rivetingly intelligent and sensitive account of the language of modern music that we can attempt such reassessments at all. Thirty years after its first publication *The Language of Modern Music* remains an essential touchstone work about modern music. If in reading it today we especially underline its passionate unflagging energies, its unshakable faith in communication and community, its deep love of and concern for music as an aesthetic and social practice, we do so with a startled awareness of how rare and helpful it still is. The total absence in it of cant and lugubrious posturing alone elevates it to the status of a classic in the field not only of musicology but of cultural studies.

I

SCHOENBERG: THE PRINCIPLE
CAPABLE OF SERVING
AS A RULE

I think one may claim that one of the main tasks that faced the creators of the New Music was *reintegration*. Perhaps it might be expressed thus, this seeking after new means of composing, of putting together:

to obtain the status of a rule; to uncover the principle capable of serving as a rule.

Those words are not mine. They are not even the words of a musician. They comprise, in fact, the definition of 'standardization' by the architect Le Corbusier,[1] a figure in modern culture of the greatest importance, not only for what he has done, for what he has built, but for what, as a creator, he stood and stands. He may be compared, not vaguely, but in close detail, with Schoenberg, with whose career and personality Le Corbusier shares an astonishing amount of common ground. (An ironic parallel resides in the sharp resistances each of these remarkable men has aroused, with the result that some of Le Corbusier's most significant and influential buildings have never risen beyond the drawing-board, while much of the music of the most influential composer of the twentieth century was for years scarcely heard in the concert hall.) Le Corbusier,

---

[1] Le Corbusier: *The Modulor*, London, 1954, p. 109.

13

out of the experience of his practice as an artist—I use the word advisedly: our ignorance of the *art* of architecture is shameful—evolved his Modulor: 'A Harmonious Measure to the Human Scale Universally applicable to Architecture and Mechanics'. Schoenberg, likewise, out of the practical business of composing, evolved his 'Method of Composing with Twelve Tones Which Are Related Only with One Another'.[1] It is amusing to compare the reception of Le Corbusier's Modulor with the reception of Schoenberg's Method. Amusing, not because the world of architecture offers a salutary contrast to that of music, but because the resistances to, the criticisms of, the Modulor—of course, one has to take into account the impact of the whole man, the total personality, just as one must with Schoenberg— are couched in the very same terms, the very language, in which the latter's Method was assaulted. We find, more-over, Le Corbusier fighting on those two fronts with which students of Schoenberg's art are so richly familiar (incidentally, Schoenberg himself tells us that he was called an architect, not to flatter him, but to deny his serial music spontaneity);[2] on the one hand Le Corbusier has had to insist that 'Science, method . . . the ART of doing things: never has it shackled talent or imprisoned the muse', on the other, to defend the Modulor from some of its indiscriminating disciples:

I have devoted watchful attention to the use of the 'Modulor', and to the supervision of its use. Sometimes I have seen on the drawing-boards designs that were displeasing, badly put together: 'But it was done with the "Modulor". '—'Well then, forget about the "Modulor". Do you imagine that the "Modulor" is a panacea for clumsiness or carelessness? Scrap it. If all you can do with the "Modulor" is to produce such horrors as these, drop it. Your eyes are your judges, the only ones you should know. Judge with your eyes, gentlemen. Let us repeat together, in simple good faith, that the "Modulor" is a working tool, a precision instrument; a keyboard shall we say, a piano, a *tuned* piano. The piano has been tuned: it is up to you to play it well. The

---

[1] Arnold Schoenberg: *Style and Idea*, London, 1951, p. 107.
[2] Schoenberg, *op. cit.*, p. 48.

New Formal Principles

"Modulor" does not confer talent, still less genius. It does not make the dull subtle: it only offers them the facility of a sure measure. But out of the unlimited choice of combinations of the "Modulor", the *choice* is yours.'[1]

Substitute 'ears' for 'eyes', 'Method' for 'Modulor', and that brilliant passage might well have been written by the musician, not by the architect. Consider these passages from Schoenberg:

The introduction of my method of composing with twelve tones does not facilitate composing; on the contrary, it makes it more difficult. Modernistically-minded beginners often think they should try it before having acquired the necessary technical equipment. This is a great mistake. The restrictions imposed on a composer by the obligation to use only one set in a composition are so severe that they can only be overcome by an imagination which has survived a tremendous number of adventures. Nothing is given by this method; but much is taken away.

The possibilities of evolving the formal elements of music—melodies, themes, phrases, motives, figures, and chords—out of a basic set are unlimited.

One has to follow the basic set; but, nevertheless, one composes as freely as before.[2]

It would hardly be necessary to recite these well-known quotations were it not for a still-widespread belief that Schoenberg's Method magically substituted an unnatural and arbitrary set of rules for what was, hitherto, the unimpeded 'inspiration' of the composer, rules which either excluded inspiration (so chained and enslaved becomes the Muse!) or made inspiration simply superfluous, i.e., the Method was a convenient recipe for composition, rather like cooking: Take a Basic Set, warm it gently until it gains shape, invert it, etc., etc.

Perhaps it was inevitable that the Method itself should become the centre of attraction. This danger was seen at the outset, when Schoenberg's 'new formal principles', in

---

[1] Le Corbusier, *op. cit.*, p. 81, pp. 130–1.
[2] Schoenberg, *op. cit.*, pp. 114, 116–17.

an essay of that title by Erwin Stein, were first set down in print—a most important paper, first published in 1924, at a time when the Method had only just reached its final stage, had just, that is, been composed (composed, *not* abstractly constructed outside musical experience).[1] Stein writes:

No doubt the chief objection to the new formal principles will be: 'Why, all this is constructed!' And so it is—not theoretically, however, but practically, not in terms of intellectual concepts but of notes. Let us see a work of man which is not constructed! Or is it seriously suggested that fugue or sonata have grown like the lilies of the field? That the Ninth 'struck' Beethoven, just as a bad joke occurs to a journalist? Why don't you have a look at his sketch-books? The constructor of genius invents.

And elsewhere he observes:

The depth and originality of Beethoven's musical ideas cannot be adequately described by such words as 'intuition' or 'inspiration'. Beethoven *worked*—not only with his heart, but also with his brain. Why, indeed, should thinking necessarily stupefy?[2]

But despite this very lucidly expressed warning, Schoenberg's Method was talked about, thought about, fought about, as if it were altogether a matter of theory. That it was deduced from his practice as a composer, then demonstrated in his serial compositions, that time and time again he begged for judgment of his work (and that of his pupils) based not upon appraisal of the Method but upon evaluation of the music as music, these facts were lost in a fog of mostly misinformed criticism. Worse still, Schoenberg's music, between the first and second world wars, made the most infrequent appearances in the concert hall, a neglect that was, of course, intensified by the ban on his music imposed by the Nazis. This quite extra-

---

[1] 'Although he constantly examined and codified his methods, he did not begin with a technique; he ended with one.' What Bruce Killeen writes of Hopkins, the poet, in 'Façade' (the *Guardian*, July 12th, 1962), is strictly applicable to Schoenberg.

[2] Erwin Stein: *Orpheus in New Guises*, London, 1953, pp. 76, 91.

ordinary and exceptional state of affairs was in no way accompanied by a diminished controversy in respect of the Method. On the contrary, we had the curious situation in which the works of certainly the most influential composer of the twentieth century were hardly to be heard, while the Method—which had first been born of the music and afterwards rationalized and adopted as a creative principle in work after work—was as hotly disputed as if the music had, in fact, been ever present in hostile ears. It was not long, indeed, before the merits of serial technique were pronounced upon by those who had had no contact with Schoenberg's music whatsoever; an oddly unreal, artificial and basically unhealthy condition which had tragic consequences for Schoenberg's personality, if not for his art. How conscious he was of the unmusical spirit in which his music was often approached could not be better illustrated than by this letter, written in his own English, which belongs to 1938:

Now one word about your intention to analyse these pieces as regards to the use of the basic set of twelve tones. I have to tell you frankly: I could not do this. It would mean that I myself had to work days to find out, how the twelve tones have been used and there are enough places where it will be almost impossible to find the solution. I myself consider this question as unimportant and have always told my pupils the same. I can show you a great number of examples, which explain the *idea* of this manner of composition, but instead of the merely mechanical application I can inform you about the compositional and esthetic advantage of it. You will accordingly realize why I call it a 'method' and why I consider the term 'system' as incorrect. Of course, you will then understand the technic [*sic*] by which this method is applied. I will give you a general aspect of the possibilities of the application and illustrate as much as possible by examples. And I expect you will acknowledge, that these works are principally works of musical imagination and not, as many suppose, mathematical constructions.[1]

One doubts whether the kind of attitude of which

---

[1] Josef Rufer: *The Works of Arnold Schoenberg*, trans. Dika Newlin, London 1962, p. 141. Letter to Arthur W. Locke, May 25th, 1938.

Thinking versus Feeling

Schoenberg complains could arise except in a period in which, as Sigfried Giedion puts it, 'thinking and feeling proceed on different levels in opposition to each other';[1] initial resistance to Schoenberg hardened into a purely intellectual reaction to what was considered to be a wholly cerebral invention (the logic of the opposition need not detain us here, though we may savour here the familiar irony of the pot calling the kettle black). Thinking excluded feeling, even on the rare occasions when one of Schoenberg's serial works was performed. It has not been so since, that is, after 1945, when many works by Schoenberg, played to a public doubtless largely innocent of— perhaps blissfully uninterested in—the Method and the interminable theoretical speeches of its opponents (and of some of its propagandists), have offered so intense an emotional experience that their audiences have insisted upon an immediate encore.[2]

Where lies the explanation of this phenomenon? No one in his senses can suppose that concert audiences in different countries, listening to different works, will have risen to their feet to celebrate the triumph of a 'system'[3] and

---

[1] Sigfried Giedion: *Space, Time and Architecture*, London, 1956, p. 13.

[2] There were a few cheers from the side-lines in advance of these welcome gains in public esteem, notably those released in *Music Survey*, a 'little' but noisy review (1947–52) which barked—and bit—on Schoenberg's behalf when it was certainly not fashionable to support his cause.

[3] 'Mine is no system but only a method, which means a *modus* of applying regularly a preconceived formula. *A method can, but need not*, be one of the consequences of a system.' Schoenberg, *op. cit.*, p. 107, n. 2. It was indeed a curiously ironic turn of events when, in February, 1958, we discovered Mr. Peter Stadlen, in an important article in *The Score* ('Serialism Reconsidered'), suggesting that the method of the Method is, after all, an illusion. Who could have guessed that the time would come when the much-abused 'strict' Method would be described thus by Mr. Stadlen: 'Far from over-determining composition—the charge usually levelled against the twelve-note system—it determines it so little as to be completely irrelevant'? I find it hard to understand how Mr. Stadlen holds this opinion in the face of so much music that, to me at least, audibly demonstrates its serial character and organization. (Why, one wonders, has one composer after another, not the most innocent class of musicians, fallen victim to the illusion?) But Mr. Stadlen has surely performed a pioneering service in draw-

demand its repeat. Of course not. What was desired was the chance immediately to renew contact with music that had deeply stirred them. No doubt, had it been possible, Schoenberg's opera, *Moses und Aron*, would have been encored after its première in Zürich in 1957; the spontaneous storm of applause was so overwhelming, so demonstrative of the profound impact the work had made, that it has lived on in the memory of those who witnessed it almost as an experience in its own right. This posthumous triumph was suggestive of the success his music might have enjoyed if it had been played more and talked about less.[1]

If Schoenberg could score a success in those very circles whose rejection of his music had always been confidently predicted by its opponents, why, one is prompted to ask, did he incur, in the first place, such unprecedented opposition?

This is a very large and complex topic, too large for the confines of this small book. It raises the question of the antagonism with which the ideas or inspirations of almost every man of genius have been greeted throughout history, in whatever sphere of human activity he has worked. We see it in music operating against composers as distinct as the conservative and socially mindful Mozart and the radical and anti-social Beethoven; the New, however it appears, has never had an easy path. Mozart eventually had to renounce the piano concerto, one of his most original

---

ing attention to some problematic aspects of serial harmony (he might concede, I think, that the Method, melodically speaking, has its points). His probings of simultaneity should be read in conjunction with the chapter of that title in George Perle's valuable *Serial Composition and Atonality*, London, 1962. (*The Score* also published some replies to Mr. Stadlen's article in its July issue of the same year and a further contribution from Mr. Stadlen in November.)

[1] Cf. the recent testimony of Artur Rubinstein (*Sunday Times*, February 11th, 1962): 'I saw [Schoenberg's] very controversial opera, *Moses und Aron*, in Paris and I was deeply impressed by its emotional impact. I didn't understand the music well; but "understand" is a word one shouldn't apply to music; there's nothing to be *understood*—for me, music must be *felt*.'

contributions to the history of music; Beethoven suffered all manner of humiliating misunderstanding and offensive commentary. Do we need to be reminded of what Louis Spohr, that highly intelligent musician, wrote about Beethoven's late music, that the last works 'became more and more eccentric, disconnected, and incomprehensible'?[1] (Spohr blamed all this on Beethoven's deafness, but how he heard the music is what matters, not his 'explanation' of its defects.) Eccentric, disconnected, incomprehensible —these were words on everybody's lips when the New Music of our own time made its appearance; and here, of course, one must think not only of Schoenberg but of Stravinsky too, and of their colleagues, Hindemith and Bartók. But whereas Beethoven, say, may have been subjected to a certain amount of that scepticism and hostility which the innovator ever merits for his daring, his music *was* performed. Spohr *heard* the ninth symphony, which he so disliked. Even a silenced Schoenberg, however, was not silent enough to pacify his critics.

The very violence of the reaction against Schoenberg tells us one thing: that in whatever cerebral or 'scientific' guise the opposition appeared, though it chose to attack the Method—as an instrument with which to beat the music—rather than the music, and eventually, through complete divorce from musical considerations, became the very intellectual exercise it supposedly condemned, there was at the back of it all a great deal of powerful, aggressive emotion. In short, Schoenberg, both the man and the musician, had hit his opponents' feelings at a very profound level, despite all appearances to the contrary. There can be no other explanation of the persistence of the resistance. Its seeming rationalization is a common enough psychological phenomenon; the more primitive the feelings, the more 'objective' the disguise they take. And if one wonders at the circuitous route by which outraged

---

[1] Sam Morgenstern (ed.): *Composers on Music*, London, 1958, p. 94.

feeling travelled, at length to emerge as 'scientific' dis-
approbation, one has to remember that the admission of
even hostile emotion towards Schoenberg would have
tended to weaken the ironic crossword or jigsaw puzzle
approach to his music. After all, if it were only a matter of
musical acrostics, where was the need for emotional
excitement?

One might, perhaps, note here, by way of refreshing
contrast, the strictly non-theoretical approach to Schoenberg's music on the part of musicians whose musicality is
not to be doubted. 'Thinking' did not impede Mahler's
generous support of his younger colleague, though he con-
fessed himself puzzled by those early works which for us
present fewer problems. His intellectual understanding
of what Schoenberg was about may have been defective,
but he had certainly felt, and felt deeply, that there was an
inspired composer at work, as it were 'behind' the puzzling
innovations.

Mahler, of course, was close to Schoenberg, who was
bound up, at least in his early years, in the same musical
environment and shared a common tradition; and let me,
upon introducing 'tradition', use Sir Herbert Read's
brilliant definition of it: 'A tradition in art is not a body of
beliefs: it is a knowledge of techniques.'[1] But even if one
takes a composer as remote from Schoenberg as Puccini,
one still meets the understanding that matters, the feeling,
as obscured as it doubtless must have been by inevitable
antipathies, that this—Puccini, in 1923, heard *Pierrot
lunaire* conducted by Schoenberg in Florence—was an
essentially *creative* voice of unusual significance. 'Who can
say that Schoenberg will not be a point of departure to a
goal in the distant future? But at present—unless I understand nothing—we are as far from a concrete artistic
realization of it as Mars is from Earth.'[2] Puccini may have

---

[1] Herbert Read: *Art Now*, London, 1948, p. 138.
[2] Mosco Carner: *Puccini, A Critical Biography*, London, 1958, p. 161.

been bewildered but he was not, it seems, hostile.[1] And there were many who, with a musical equipment which could not be mentioned in the same breath as Puccini's, *were* prepared to say outright that the idea of Schoenberg as a 'point of departure to a goal in the distant future' was both ludicrous and lunatic.

If we take another pair of composers we shall find that the creators of the New Music have not been without their patrons (significantly enough either senior composers or practitioners from the other arts; only rarely does one encounter an enlightened critic). Debussy stood in relation to Stravinsky somewhat as Mahler stood to Schoenberg. When thanking Stravinsky for his gift of the score of *Le Sacre du printemps* Debussy wrote, '. . . it is not necessary to tell you of the joy I had to see my name associated with a very beautiful thing that with the passage of time will be more beautiful still. For me, who descend the other slope of the hill but keep, however, an intense passion for music, for me it is a special satisfaction to tell you how much you have *enlarged the boundaries of the permissible in the empire of sound.*' (My italics.) That brilliant phrase, which so succinctly sums up an important part, at least, of the achievement of the New Music, belongs to a letter written by Debussy in November, 1913, only a few months after the work's stormy première in Paris. But he had already responded positively to the significance of *Le Sacre* at an earlier stage, when indeed he had tried the work through with Stravinsky at the piano. He refers to that occasion thus: 'Our reading at the piano of *Le Sacre du printemps* . . . is always present in my mind. It haunts me like a *beautiful nightmare* and I try, in vain, to re-invoke the terrific impression.'[2] (My italics.) 'Beautiful nightmare'!

---

[1] He showed, too, characteristic perceptiveness in the case of Stravinsky, who writes in his *Expositions and Developments*, London, 1962, p. 137, that Puccini 'had told Diaghilev and others that my music was horrible, but that it was also very talented'.

[2] See Igor Stravinsky and Robert Craft: *Conversations with Igor Stravinsky*, London, 1959, pp. 50, 52.

That striking comment seems to me to contain a world of truth in it; for Debussy, I suspect, must have found *Le Sacre* disturbing (like a nightmare) and yet his profound musicality enabled him to assimilate the experience, to respond creatively to the disturbance. Hence the paradox of the 'beautiful' nightmare, which in fact is no paradox but a wonderfully exact expression of conflicting feelings resolved in a synthesis.

Debussy's and Mahler's sympathies were outshone in width by Schoenberg's, whose judgments were unpredictable but always extraordinarily positive—he had a nose for talent which rarely betrayed him, however remote one would have thought the possibility of contact: think of his improbable commendation of Charles Ives, of Gershwin,[1] of his comment upon Sibelius and Shostakovich—'I feel they have the breath of symphonists.'[2]

But of course the reactions of Mahler or Debussy to the New Music must be treated as special cases. It is not necessarily the positive response of men of genius which creates the conditions in which the New may flourish. I think it is profoundly interesting that at least two of the senior composers out of whose works the New Music itself was born should have so explicitly taken the side of the younger generation, should have sensed the emergent New

---

[1] Morgenstern, *op. cit.*, pp. 384–6.

[2] Schoenberg, *op. cit.*, p. 195. Stravinsky has proved to be less tolerant of composers who do not fit into the framework of his own criteria for evaluation. But there are admirably independent judgments of his, none the less, which are somehow all the more impressive because the music praised is often alien to Stravinsky's mode of thinking. An example is his unexpectedly favourable comment upon Mahler: 'I am glad that young musicians today have come to appreciate the lyric gift in the songs of the composer [Richard] Strauss despised, and who is more significant in our music than he is: Gustav Mahler.' (*Conversations*, p. 75.) That Stravinsky's ears have caught the significance of Mahler, despite what one would have thought irreconcilable differences of musical character, is not only evidence that he can recognize the New even in a tradition which he finds largely uncongenial but also a telling example of what is too rarely encountered among the professional appraisers of art: a judgment which has conquered personal inclinations in taste or fashion.

and rightly valued it. (We must remember, however, that Mahler died in 1911, Debussy in 1918. There was still a lot of the New to come!) But it would be silly to overlook the very many who took the other side and were vehemently opposed to the New, not all of them, by any means, men of ill will or uncultured or unmusical. It would be equally silly to credit everyone with the ears of a Debussy or a Mahler. As we have seen, Mahler himself was not able to avoid confessions of mystification despite his unreserved support and encouragement of Schoenberg; and Debussy, in letters *not* addressed to Stravinsky himself, spoke of his younger colleague in terms—'a young savage', for example —which disclose a certain ambiguity of attitude.[1] If Mahler and Debussy had their difficulties, small wonder that less open and less gifted ears found the going hard.

That it should take time for those enlargements of the 'boundaries of the permissible in the empire of sound' to

---

[1] See, for instance, the letters quoted in Victor I. Seroff: *Debussy. Musician of France*, London, 1957, pp. 311, 332. Stravinsky writes, 'After reading [Debussy's] friendly and commendatory letters to me (he liked *Petroushka* very much) I was puzzled to find quite a different feeling concerning my music in some of his letters to his musical friends of the same period.' 'Was it duplicity,' Stravinsky asks, 'or was he annoyed at his incapacity to digest the music of the *Sacre* when the younger generation enthusiastically voted for it?' Surely, neither? I do not doubt Debussy's admiration of Stravinsky's music; nor do I doubt his resistance to it. Somewhere he must have felt that he was being 'replaced' by the younger man; hence, no doubt, the feelings which seem to contradict the explicit admiration. But in fact the contradiction is more apparent than real. We must simply understand that one set of feelings does not exclude another. In a sense, Debussy's positive response is the more genuine because of the latent hostility he had to overcome. It is a pattern that recurs throughout musical history. Stravinsky (*Conversations*, p. 48) is needlessly surprised.

In any event, composers, unlike critics, have no duty to try to understand composers. On the contrary, self-preservation will often dictate a composer's dislike of a colleague, dead or alive. The classic expression of the composer's fear of influence or replacement by the New belongs to Rimsky-Korsakov, who said of Debussy's music, 'Better not listen—one runs the risk of getting accustomed to his music, and one would end by liking it!'. (Quoted in Eric Walter White: *Stravinsky: A Critical Survey*, London, 1947, p. 16.) A strictly realistic attitude for a composer, one might add. It is only when a critic adopts it, who may listen to the music, but with his prejudices not with his ears, that it becomes strictly immoral.

be assimilated by a wider public than a small band of progressive composers and sympathetic artists—it is interesting how often, in this respect, the practitioner of another art is in advance of the musician—occasions no surprise. Such has always been the case throughout musical history. The 'new sound symbolizing a new personality'[1] encounters strenuous opposition before winning final acceptance. And acceptance *is* the ultimate stage achieved: even in so tumultuous a century as our own many of the new sounds created by the new personalities, after fierce preliminary battles, have now become part of the aural establishment of musicians and music-lovers; one need only think of the success enjoyed by Hindemith, of the reputation achieved by Bartók's string quartets (not to speak of the comparative popularity of his violin concerto or Concerto for Orchestra), of the world audience that each new work by Stravinsky commands. This is not to say that understanding of these major figures in twentieth-century music is necessarily complete. On the other hand one cannot say that they have not now been received.

But these three composers, though their eminent positions may have been consolidated since 1945, were all successful before the outbreak of the second world war. There were, of course, heart-breaking difficulties and misunderstandings—perhaps Bartók suffered most in this respect—and I have no wish to underestimate the courage these artists displayed in the face of determined criticism. But their music *was* played, and, however slowly, it gained the admiration of a public which grew ever wider. It is against the background of the relative inter-war success of three out of four major composers in the history of music in our time that we must consider the exceptional case of the fourth, Schoenberg, whose art enjoyed nothing like the degree of recognition accorded that of his colleagues.

---

[1] Schoenberg: *Harmonielehre*, Vienna, fourth edition, n.d., p. 479.

A Changed Climate

I have already suggested that the quite recent past has witnessed a radical change in attitude to Schoenberg's music. Comparative statistics are particularly revealing. His Variations for Orchestra, op. 31, is a work central to our understanding of his music, and central, one might add, to our understanding of much important music composed under his influence. (I shall have something to say later of the curious way in which Schoenberg's works have exerted a powerful influence upon the art of composition while remaining virtually unperformed.) Between 1928 and 1948 there were twelve performances of this piece. Between 1949 and 1957: eighty-eight! There is quite a slice of musical history bound up in those figures.[1] Indeed, they were indicative of a vital swing in taste. A revolution, in fact. As I write, I have to hand the prospectus of the Promenade Concerts (!) for 1962. It states: 'The largest attendance of the whole [1961] season was for a programme which included Schoenberg's Violin Concerto.' Is revolution too strong a word?

Better late than never. But why so delayed? Why did Schoenberg's 'new sounds' take longer than any other composer's to achieve acceptance? The delay may even seem paradoxical when one considers that the sensitivity of Schoenberg's ear meant that many of his most novel sonorities were far more considerate of sheer beauty of sound than, say, many 'barbarities' perpetrated by Bartók or Stravinsky at their most strenuously dissonant. Can the time-lag be explained by the cultural vacuum created in Europe by the Nazis? That political catastrophe undoubtedly played a rôle in hindering the advance of the New. But we must remember that the Nazi censorship hit not only Schoenberg but also Hindemith, not to speak of Stravinsky, Bartók, Berg and Webern, all of whose music came under the ban. And despite this impediment, as I have already suggested, the music of Schoenberg's col-

---

[1] They come from an information sheet published by Universal Edition in the spring of 1958.

leagues made headway while his did not. (Webern, of course, suffered an even more rigorous stifling than his master—*one* performance of his Concerto, op. 24, between 1935 and 1946: sixty-three between 1947 and 1957. Since his music represented an intensification of aspects of Schoenberg's Method which, even in the milder form practised by their originator, attracted a quite special measure of ill repute, the more complete suppression of Webern requires no further comment at this stage.) It may be that a useful sense of guilt at past misdeeds has helped along performances of Schoenberg's music since 1945, particularly, perhaps, in Germany. But I doubt whether, in fact, the overt political ban made all that difference. Performances, I believe, would have been minimal even in the absence of an official interdict.

To what then may we attribute the arousing of resistances to Schoenberg's music, since it would appear that in very many respects his art presented difficulties not more sizeable than those unfolded by, say, Stravinsky or Bartók? What was it about the New Music,[1] as practised by

---

[1] Schoenberg had no love for this term. A 'battle-cry' was his description of it, and he continues: 'A battle-cry must, perhaps, be superficial and at least partially wrong if it is to gain popularity. . . . *What is New Music?* Evidently it must be music which, though it is still music, differs in all essentials from previously composed music. Evidently, in higher art, only that is worth being presented which has never before been presented', etc., etc. Schoenberg's irony at the expense of the newly fashionable and frivolous is revealing of his responsible attitude to the question of originality. I need hardly say that I do not employ the term New Music in the sense pilloried by Schoenberg. For me it is merely a convenient and I think valid manner of referring to the movements in music which we recognize in the achievements of Schoenberg, Stravinsky, Bartók and Hindemith as surely as we recognize the New Architecture in the buildings of Walter Gropius or Le Corbusier or the New Art in the radical works of Picasso and his colleagues. Schoenberg (*Style and Idea*, pp. 38–9) was right to chastise the camp-followers of the New Music who simply indulged in all manner of extravagances for the sake of sensation and self-advertisement. But this sort of feverish frivolity always surrounds inventions and innovations of real significance. Arnold Hauser, in his *Social History of Art*, London, 1951, Vol. II, p. 871, makes a good point when he writes that the 'rapid development of technology'—characteristic of the end of the nineteenth century and the beginning of the twentieth—'not only accelerates the change of fashion, but also the shifting emphases in the criteria of aesthetic taste;

Schoenberg, that seemed to earn it a ferocity of denunciation spared his colleagues?

This is a complicated question which must, I think, be answered—or an answer attempted—in several stages, though I believe the conclusion may be stated in advance of the working-out: that it was the misunderstanding of the serial Method itself which contributed most to the postponement of appreciation of Schoenberg's music. But the Method did not finally crystallize until the early 1920s, and Schoenberg had been busy as a composer since well before the turn of the century. His first wholly serial work, the Suite for piano, op. 25, was not completed until 1923. If it was the *Method* which aroused particular resistance, what about the large amount of pre-serial music he wrote before then? And in reply we have to admit that here, too, Schoenberg's music met with not just a negative response but very active hostility.

But I think that there is an important difference in the reactions to Schoenberg's pre-serial music and the reactions against his Method. The earlier opposition, painful as it may have been for the composer, at least had the merit of retaining some sort of touch with musical reality. The music had been experienced, if only to be rejected. This was not the case later, when the Method was endlessly debated but the music was unplayed. Indeed, in a sense, the angry condemnations of Schoenberg's pre-serial works seem to me to be natural. The passing of the years tends to obliterate keen memory of the nature of his innovations in the first decade of the twentieth century. Already, by 1908, we have the second string quartet, in the finale of which Schoenberg, as it were, composed in music of memorable beauty his renunciation of tonality. Today, perhaps, when

it often brings about a senseless and fruitless mania for innovation, a restless striving for the new for the mere sake of novelty'. Likewise, the rapid developments in the arts which we have under review were accompanied by outbreaks of novelty for novelty's sake which tended to give the New Music a bad name among the indiscriminating. It is only today that Schoenberg's *New Music* has become an unhappy reality.

the works from Schoenberg's non-tonal period no longer bewilder the ear, however much they may excite the imagination, we may too readily forget the incredible impact these pieces must have made on their first audiences—in some cases over fifty years ago.

There were many who thought Schoenberg had stepped right outside the bounds of musical sanity. It speaks for the composer's courage that he never faltered in his belief in his inspiration, though only too well aware of how his exploration of new territories would be received. He did not have to remind himself that his op. 4, the string sextet *Verklärte Nacht*, which raised none of the problems of the later non-tonal pieces, was refused a first performance by a Viennese musical society because of 'the "revolutionary" use of one—that is *one* single uncatalogued dissonance'.[1] So Schoenberg knew what to expect; and the expected happened.

But what is interesting is how, on the whole, non-tonal music has succeeded in riding the storm. The confusion and criticism of musicians and listeners faced with the relinquishment of tonality has proved to be of that variety of opposition which always first greets the New and then gradually evaporates. We see this dissolution of hostility if we look at the comparative popularity of a primarily non-tonal work like Berg's *Wozzeck*, which has made its way in the world with surprising ease, has triumphed, indeed, over all its antagonists.[2] Or we may take earlier precedents, like the most advanced and progressive things in Richard Strauss's *Elektra* and *Salome* (*Elektra*, especially), highly original and impressive clutches at the future—they undoubtedly influenced not only Berg but also Schoenberg, in *Erwartung*—which at first met strenuous resistance but were soon assimilated by the initially outraged ear. How deeply ironical it is that *Erwartung*, out of which *Wozzeck* sprang—often note for note—was not performed

---

[1] Schoenberg, *Style and Idea*, p. 189.

[2] But how increasingly tonal it sounds these days!

until 1924, not so many months before the première of *Wozzeck*, though Schoenberg had completed the composition of his monodrama in September, 1909. It is this kind of incredible time-lag between the act of composition and first performance of many of Schoenberg's works which could create chaos in the chronology of his influence on the course of twentieth-century music. We have continually to remember that his influence was radiated outwards by study of his scores by other composers, by his pupils above all, who in their own music promoted what were, in effect, characteristically Schoenbergian inventions and ideas. But the 'originals' from which the 'models' were derived were not recognized, because unknown: because unplayed. There has not been another case of 'influence' like this in the whole history of music.

The works I have chosen to illustrate the relative swiftness with which non-tonal music gained acceptance, make a point or two about the special features associated with this development in our century. The glance *back* to Richard Strauss is itself significant. We may express our first point thus:

Non-tonal music was a natural evolution for which the listener, however unconsciously, had been prepared by the increasing enfeeblement of functional tonality towards the end of the nineteenth century.

A second point is dependent upon the nature of the music by Berg and Strauss that I have mentioned. Dramatic works, it will be noticed. How often musical drama proves to carry the burden of the New! We may say:

The text (or book)—the consequent dramatic organization— has acted as a powerfully integrative element in music which precipitated the abandonment of tonality, enabling the composer to maintain a grasp on immediate comprehensibility at one level while daring to introduce on the other what was bound to be felt as a surrender to anarchy.

Thus does the listener benefit from the composer ensuring

himself against doubts of the propriety of his own creative daemon. For there is no mistaking the crisis of conscience the responsible artist must suffer when initiating a departure from tradition so radical as Schoenberg's. In these necessarily exacting circumstances a song-text or opera libretto will often be the means by which the composer launches himself out into a new world of sound. The subject of *Elektra* objectified and validated Strauss's emancipated dissonances; they could at first be understood through the drama, then comprehended musically. It is against this background that we can fully appreciate the setting of Stefan George's poem, *Entrückung*, as the pioneering finale of Schoenberg's second string quartet. The famous first line of the poem runs:

> *Ich fühle luft von anderem planeten.*
> (I feel the air from another planet.)

There could scarcely be a clearer example of the New in music calling in words as an auxiliary in the cause of comprehensibility.[1]

Point three:
The abandonment of tonality abjures rather than asserts.

By which I mean not to criticize Schoenberg's non-tonal works as purely negative gestures, which they most certainly are not, but to isolate the real difference in principle between the positive assertion comprised in the serial Method, and the character of non-tonality, which affirmed the *absence* of tonality and, despite the achievement of individual works, could make no claims as a technique of composition. That it could not, was, as Schoenberg was the first to see, a weakness—'New colourful harmony was

---

[1] Schoenberg himself writes (*op. cit.*, p. 106): 'A little later, i.e., post 1908, I discovered how to construct larger forms by following a text or poem. The differences in size and shape of its parts and the change in character and mood were mirrored in the shape and size of the composition, in its dynamics and tempo, figuration and accentuation, instrumentation and orchestration. Thus the parts were differentiated as clearly as they had formerly been by the tonal and structural functions of harmony.'

offered; but much was lost': [1] hence the eventual unfolding of the Method, after the long period of experiment and exploration which succeeded what we may now view as a passing phase devoted to non-tonality.

What undoubtedly left Schoenberg dissatisfied with non-tonality, even when he himself, in many unique works, had conquered the compositional problems it set, must, I think, be viewed as an essentially negative feature of this style. Schoenberg wrote that the innovation of non-tonality 'like every innovation, destroys while it produces'. [2] One may grant the destruction and the need for it, but question the sufficiency of the product. Non-tonality, in fact, did not produce *enough* by way of compensation for the loss of tonality.

The Method, on the other hand, created the possibility of a language of music, of a 'standardization'. To return to the phrase of Le Corbusier's which defines that latter term, with which I opened this book:

Standardization: to obtain the status of a rule; to uncover the principle capable of serving as a rule.

This question of standardization, of the rule, touches very nearly upon one of the main reasons why the Method excited such opposition. By way of paradoxical contrast, the absence of the rule, of standardization, in non-tonal music, made the path of such music easier: it is less difficult, speaking both psychologically and aurally, finally to assimilate what abjures than what asserts, the distinction I have drawn between non-tonality and the Method. And I think there are ample concrete examples of particular works which support this inference. We need not, perhaps, stick to non-tonality. If we move out to the wider sphere of anti-tonality—anti-constructive tonality—which would include music by Debussy or Stravinsky, we find there the same situation obtaining, i.e., initial be-

---

[1] Schoenberg, *op. cit.*, p. 105.
[2] Ibid.

wilderment and hostility succeeded by relatively swift acceptance.

But Schoenberg's non-tonal works did not win acceptance any more speedily than did his serial compositions. Why not?

The answer, I believe, falls into two parts. One, perhaps the more important, attaches to the Method, which retrospectively influenced attitudes to the non-tonal period; but this complex subject I should like to delay awhile. The second is very much bound up with the character of the works Schoenberg produced at this time, that is between 1907 and the early 1920s.

There is an immediate point to be made about the outward character of Schoenberg's non-tonal works. Many of them are purely *instrumental*. I have already suggested that non-tonal music in celebrated instances—and like many another innovation in music—availed itself of a song-text or libretto as accomplice in launching new worlds of sound. We have seen that Schoenberg himself floated into non-tonality in the finale of his second string quartet, as it were, on the wings of George's words. We have his own testimony to the importance of the text for the organization of large-scale works written in a non-tonal style.[1] But it is characteristic of Schoenberg's personality that very early in his non-tonal period he was busy with instrumental compositions, with the Three Pieces for Piano, op. 11, the Five Pieces for Orchestra, op. 16, and the Six Pieces for Piano, op. 19, accomplishing in the instrumental field what he felt was accomplished in that remarkable cycle of songs, *Das Buch der hängenden Gärten*:

. . . I have succeeded for the first time in approaching an ideal of expression and form that had hovered before me for some years. Hitherto I had not sufficient strength and sureness to realize that ideal. Now, however, that I have definitely started on my journey, I may confess to having broken off the bonds of a bygone aesthetic; and if I am striving towards a goal that seems to me certain, nevertheless

[1] See n. 1 above, p. 31.

I already feel the opposition that I shall have to overcome. I feel also with what heat even those of the feeblest temperament will reject my works, and I suspect that even those who have hitherto believed in me will not be willing to perceive the necessity of this development.[1]

What keen insight Schoenberg had into the reception of his 'ideal'! But his creative daemon drove him on, on and into the very field where the application of non-tonality posed the most critical compositional problems and virtually guaranteed non-comprehension from the audience. That he himself realized that non-tonal *instrumental* music ran special perils of misunderstanding is confirmed by the titles—dropped later—which first adorned the Five Pieces for Orchestra, titles which were not programmatic in intent but, rather, presented musical facts, e.g., 'Das obligate Rezitativ' (the 'Obbligato Recitative') or 'Der wechselnde Akkord' (the 'Changing Chord'), or a hint of the predominant mood, e.g., 'Vorgefühl' ('Presentiment') or 'Vergangenes' ('Bygones'), as points of reference around which the listener's understanding might crystallize.

There can be no doubt that the immediacy of Schoenberg's introduction of non-tonality into the instrumental sphere, tribute though it is to his extraordinary capacity to roll several historical stages into one, i.e., the simultaneous development of non-tonality in 'dramatic' and 'absolute' music, meant quite irrevocably that in these years, in this field, he was simply ahead of his time; for once, the threadbare image succinctly depicts an actual situation.

It was improbable, then, that the non-tonal instrumental works would enjoy the relative success scored by *Pierrot lunaire* where, once again, the 'three times seven' texts were a distinct aid to comprehensibility; and, be it noted, the innovation for which this work is, above all, notorious, the introduction of the *Sprechstimme* ('Speaking Voice'), was emphatically on the side of quick comprehen-

---

[1] Quoted in Dika Newlin: *Bruckner, Mahler, Schoenberg,* New York, 1947, pp. 235–6. The première of the song-cycle took place in Vienna on January 14th, 1910, in connection with which event Schoenberg made the statement quoted above.

sion. All that Erwin Stein writes about the *Sprechstimme* is, of course, true, that 'without turning into actual song, the sound of speech either dominates the ensemble, or else participates in it on equal footing', that 'what is new about Schoenberg's spoken melody is that its character, expression and mood are as strong, and at the same time as closely defined, as if it were sung or played—in a word, that speech becomes music';[1] but though speech does indeed become music, the audibility of speech is retained. In a word, in fact, in *Pierrot lunaire* one hears the words. This asset, naturally, is part of the inspiration of the *Sprechstimme*, which offered a novel solution of a problem —the mixture of speech and music—that had both fascinated and defeated composers for centuries. There is no doubt that in this case, as in few others, Schoenberg's innovation actively contributed to the speed with which *Pierrot lunaire* travelled after its première in 1912—'for the first time, Schoenberg's fame was beginning to spread to foreign lands'.[2]

He once wrote: 'Composition with twelve tones has no other aim than comprehensibility',[3] but the same aim, no less certainly, accounts for a major part of the intention which promoted the invention of the *Sprechstimme*, which managed to be both new *and* readily assimilable; its newness, in fact, rested in the clarification it brought to textures rent, hitherto, by incompatible components: speech *versus* music. Perhaps the clarifying, pacifying property of the *Sprechstimme* scores its greatest triumph in *Moses und Aron*, where Schoenberg showed that it was possible to combine *Sprech-* and *Singstimme* to their mutual advantage, not destruction. The text, indeed, is more audible in either part of this novel combination than in the customary vocal duet. (Cf. Act I, Scene 2, of the opera.)

Pierrot lunaire fared better than almost any other work from Schoenberg's non-tonal period, but perhaps for

---

[1] Stein, *op. cit.*, p. 86.   [2] Newlin, *op. cit.*, p. 248.   [3] Schoenberg, *op. cit.*, p. 103.

rather special reasons; and its case remained untypical. I have suggested why the instrumental works created particular problems of comprehensibility which, to some degree at least, were avoided—or, for the listener, by-passed—in those works where texts functioned like maps. I have not, I hope, underestimated the fact that the New always encounters resistance, nor neglected the *size* of Schoenberg's break with the 'bygone aesthetic'. These factors, however, singly or united, do not offer anything like a complete explanation of the solid—or nearly solid—wall of opposition which confronted his non-tonal music. Or to put it another way: do not explain why the chinks in the wall, like the break-through achieved by *Pierrot lunaire*, did not develop into breaches which would eventually have brought the wall down.

The difficulty of mastering a new means of musical expression is not, cannot be, the explanation. There are too many precedents in history to confirm the acceptance of the New after however intense a rejection.

Perhaps it is in the mastering of new feelings that we meet the problem of resistance to Schoenberg's music at its most profound level. This topic, however, is relevant not only to Schoenberg but also to Stravinsky, to the practitioners of the New, indeed, in all the arts, whether painting, architecture, or literature.

Sigfried Giedion has much to say that is pertinent. He writes how, through the work of the artist, 'new parts of the world are made accessible to feeling' and continues:

The opening up of . . . new realms of feeling has always been the artist's chief mission. A great deal of our world would lack all emotional significance if it were not for his work. As recently as the eighteenth century, mountain scenery was felt to exhibit nothing except a formless and alarming confusion. Winckelmann, the discoverer of Greek art, could not bear to look out of the windows of his carriage when he crossed the Alps into Italy, around 1760. He found the jumbled granite masses of the St. Gotthard so frightful that he pulled down the blinds and sat back to await the smooth outlines of the Italian countryside. A century later, Ruskin was seeking out the mountains of Chamonix as a refuge from an industrial world that made no kind of aesthetic sense. Ships, bridges, iron constructions—the new artistic potentialities of his period, in short—these were the things Ruskin pulled down the blinds on. Right now there are great areas of our experience which are still waiting to be claimed by feeling. Thus we are no longer limited to seeing objects from the distances normal for earth-bound animals. The bird's-eye view has opened up to us whole new aspects of the world. Such new modes of perception carry with them new feelings which the artist must formulate.[1]

Giedion is a historian of architecture; but what he promotes as the artist's significant mission, 'the opening up of . . . new realms of feeling', seems to me to be wholly applicable to music, to be, in fact, a highly important aspect of the New Music.

One must appreciate, too, Giedion's bold and imaginative conception of the artist functioning 'a great deal like an inventor or a scientific discoverer: all three seek new relations between man and his world'. But possibly he tends to view the task of the artist too exclusively as a matter of finding the new expressive means to match the 'new modes of perception' (from whatever field of discovery). I do not doubt that this extraordinarily fascinating cross-fertilization between the arts and the sciences, and between the arts themselves, does take place; that a period does have a unity of feeling about it, difficult—or impossible—as it may be to define; that, as Giedion himself writes, 'Techniques, sciences, the arts—all these are carried on by men who have grown up together in the same period, exposed to its characteristic influences. The feelings which it is the special concern of the artist to express are also at work within the engineer and the mathematician. This emotional background shared by such otherwise divergent pursuits is what we must try to discover.' But what Giedion does not, I think, sufficiently stress is the frequency with which the artist himself unfolds the 'new modes of perception' and at the same time creates the new

---

[1] Giedion, *op. cit.*, p. 426, pp. 427–8.

means with which to express them. Indeed, very often these two processes are absolutely inseparable—there is no 'discovery' without the new style to match it. For a clear example of an artist uncovering a new mode of perception which was radically to influence architecture, design (of numberless utility objects we see about us every day) and construction, an example, in short, of the artist opening up new ways of feeling not only for art but also for technology, we need only look to Cubism, the invention of a painter, Picasso, or perhaps of a group of painters whose common groping towards a new technique crystallized in the person of Picasso, a technique which in many significant respects makes it a phenomenon comparable to Schoenberg's invention of the serial Method. But more of this later. We may also, while on this topic of the artist as leader, as pathfinder, recall Freud's admiration of the many writers—poets or novelists—who had anticipated his own discoveries. Ernest Jones writes:

[Freud] evidently felt an affinity between himself and imaginative writers, though he admired, and perhaps somewhat envied, the facility with which they could reach a piece of insight that had cost him much labour to achieve. They were wonderful people. 'One may heave a sigh [wrote Freud] at the thought that it is vouchsafed to a few, with hardly an effort, to salve from the whirlpool of their emotions the deepest truths, to which we others have to force our way, ceaselessly groping amid torturing uncertainties.'[1]

There speaks the innovating scientist who followed in the steps of the innovating artist!

The introduction of Freud into my text is fortuitous but relevant. After all, not only must he take an honoured and substantial place in the ranks of the founder-fathers of the New—widening our concept of the New to embrace spheres other than music, painting or architecture—but the very nature of his achievement, what he discovered about the unconscious mind, does, I think, bear a particular relation to important features of works from

---

[1] Ernest Jones: *Sigmund Freud: Life and Work*, Vol. III, London, 1957, p. 449.

Schoenberg's non-tonal period. I must at once insist that I am not doing more than to suggest that here we have an example of what Giedion has in mind when he writes of a common 'emotional background' shared by 'otherwise divergent pursuits'. I am not saying that Schoenberg was a musical Freud. One rightly suspects such easy equations. I would prefer to underline the divergences than to promote a dubious parallel; but at the same time the fact remains, and it is, I think, a fact, that in the years when Freud was diving into—and uncovering—the Unconscious, so too was Schoenberg; because in a very real sense, having abandoned tonality, and with it the 'subconsciously functioning *sense of form* which gave a real composer an almost somnambulistic sense of security in creating, with utmost precision, the most delicate distinctions of formal elements',[1] Schoenberg had only his Unconscious to look to as potential source of the means and principles of unity and organization which would replace the lost paradise of tonality. In the context of his exceptionally brave plunge into unknown territory, these words of Schoenberg have particular force: 'One must be convinced of the infallibility of one's own fantasy and one must believe in one's own inspiration.'[2] Perhaps one might substitute Unconscious for 'inspiration' in the second half of the sentence. Certainly Schoenberg had to believe in *his*, in his non-tonal period, and certainly his Unconscious did not let him down. Indeed, unique works from these years were born of a fantastic marriage of Schoenberg's prodigious talent to his Unconscious.

Two works which seem to me to be patent offspring of this remarkable union are the Five Pieces for Orchestra and the monodrama *Erwartung*. The Five Pieces—strange to relate—were first performed in London in the Queen's Hall by Sir Henry Wood in September, 1912, for which occasion (it was the world première, not simply the first

---

[1] Schoenberg, *op. cit.*, p. 106.　　[2] Ibid.

English performance) the following note appeared in the
programme by way of elucidation:

This music seeks to express all that dwells in us subconsciously like
a dream; which is a great fluctuant power, and is built upon none of
the lines that are familiar to us; which has a rhythm, as the blood has
its pulsating rhythm, as all life in us has its rhythm; which has a
tonality, but only as the sea or the storm has its tonality; which has
harmonies, though we cannot grasp or analyze them nor can we trace
its themes. All its technical craft is submerged, made one and indivi-
sible with the content of the work.[1]

These words were not Schoenberg's; on the contrary,
they are identical with a passage in a polemical pamphlet
by Walter Krug, which was generally hostile to Schoenberg, if Berg's assessment of it is to be believed.[2] But
despite this paradoxical situation, the sense of the passage
might have helped—or at least was intended to help—
English ears of 1912 to receive an altogether novel
experience. There is no denying, I think, that Schoenberg,
in his Five Pieces and *Erwartung*—in the latter, perhaps,
even more explicitly—did explore areas of feeling new to
music, thus fulfilling one of the most important rôles of the
artist assigned him by Giedion, 'the opening up of . . . new
realms of feeling', while at the same time he relied to an
astounding degree upon the 'infallibility of his own fantasy' as guarantee of the works' integral form. It is true,
of course, that in certain compositions from these non-
tonal years Schoenberg adopted, as means of organization,
of continuation, established forms or contrapuntal textures. There is the great Passacaglia, 'Nacht', in *Pierrot
lunaire*, for example, or the brilliantly audible canonic
texture of 'Parodie', in the same work. On the other hand,
there are also many instances of Schoenberg searching out
new principles of unity, e.g., the 'Changing Chord' of the

---

[1] Quoted in Nicolas Slonimsky: *Music Since 1900*, third edition, New York,
1949, pp. 127-8.

[2] See Willi Reich: *Alban Berg*, London, 1965, pp. 223-5.

third of the Five Pieces. All these varied means of securing *comprehensibility* were explicit on Schoenberg's part and recognizable for the listener. The Passacaglia in *Pierrot lunaire* is unlike the Rondo of Webern's string trio which, as Stravinsky writes, 'is wonderfully interesting but no one hears it as a Rondo'.[1]

These insistent reminders of the need for something to replace that 'subconsciously functioning *sense of form*' hitherto provided by tonality, whether derived from tradition or newly devised, were profoundly typical of Schoenberg's creative character, of his efforts to 'uncover the principle capable of serving as a rule'. We see the search for the rule in many aspects of the non-tonal works, but at the same time—and sometimes in the same work—we encounter a method of composition which can only be described as 'free': which is not to say that these works are anarchical, but that their undoubted unity and organization remain stubbornly resistant to analysis. There have been attempts to demonstrate the constructive principles which supposedly underpin the structure of *Erwartung*, for example,[2] but they have scarcely proved successful; on the contrary, they seem to me to cloud what is a clear if singular issue, that we are confronted in *Erwartung* with a work which, as Mr. Hans Keller precisely puts it, 'develops according to unconscious laws'; and he adds, 'the honest amongst us analysts have to admit that we have not yet discovered a great deal about them'.[3] *Erwartung*, in fact, is the perfect example of what I have in mind as the result of Schoenberg marrying his talent to his Unconscious. But the union, of course, however fruitful artistically speaking, represents one of the principal reasons for the non-tonal works' slow progress: the projec-

---

[1] *Conversations*, p. 126.

[2] See Walter and Alexander Goehr: 'Arnold Schönberg's Development towards the Twelve-Note System', in *European Music in the Twentieth Century*, ed. Howard Hartog, London, 1957, pp. 89–92.

[3] Hans Keller: 'Erwartung', in *Guide to the Holland Festival*, 1958, pp. 24–6.

tion, in music, of unconscious forces hit people hard when it aroused feelings in them to which they were unaccustomed, often painful feelings I think one must confess—it is not every pair of ears which, like Debussy's, can react to the New as a '*beautiful* nightmare'—and the ensuing censorship, suppression, of these disturbing feelings, outwards turned, became, as is a common enough psychological event, an instrument of criticism of the composer; 'projection', in fact, in the strict psycho-analytical sense of the term. I have no doubt that here we are at the very heart of the resistance to the music of Schoenberg's non-tonal period. So new and, I think, so narrow (I must qualify this word later) were the 'new realms of feeling' opened up by Schoenberg, perhaps most explicitly in *Erwartung* but, to my ears, no less obviously in the Five Pieces, that he was obliged to conquer not only immense problems of musical language and organization but, far more difficult—indeed, one may wonder whether Schoenberg realized to the full what he was attempting—to overcome deep-founded emotional prejudice and hostility, seemingly based upon objective reaction against his 'revolutionary' style but founded in fact in powerful emotions released or probed by the music, feelings which were at length transformed and turned against the composer, as I have described above.

I have some reservations to make about certain of these non-tonal works. Their depth appears to me self-evident. It is their width, if it may be so described, which worries me, which, I believe, has been one valid reason for the slowness of their progress in public esteem, which, I think, may well limit their appeal even when, as has now surely evolved, we have a state of affairs where the genius which informs them is readily conceded. I think my concept of 'narrowness' may best be approached if we look first for some other examples of new territories of feeling which, slightly to reslant Giedion's phrase, have been made 'accessible to *music*'.

The list could be a substantial one. A few instances which immediately come to mind are suggestive of the widely contrasted composers—in type and chronology—who have introduced 'new modes of perception' and the new means with which to express them. To take a famous example, Beethoven and the *alla marcia* section in the finale of his ninth symphony—one of the first and certainly most inspired and original appearances in music of what one might term sublime banality, the use of popular materials in the service of the most exalted aims. Controversy about this passage continues to this very day; proof enough, if proof were needed, of the singular emotional tension which the march generates: as late as 1955 Dr. Gordon Jacob can write of 'this great movement which covers the whole gamut from the sublime to the ridiculous, the latter being represented by the *alla marcia* section . . .'.[1] It is profoundly significant of the innovating character of the march that there are still plenty of people about who can't stomach it. Beethoven wrote his ninth symphony in 1822–24. Let us not be too surprised, then, at some of the delayed comprehension to which Schoenberg has been subjected. A parallel may be drawn here quite meaningfully. It is the presence of new feeling, as much in Beethoven's march as in Schoenberg's *Erwartung*, which arouses opposition. We dislike what we fear. Beethoven's march continues to frighten some cultivated ears over a century after the passage was composed—and I use 'frighten' advisedly, for fear, I believe, is what the resistance to it boils down to, or up from, however much it may be rationalized in the guise of offended good taste.

This one aspect alone of Beethoven's tremendous finale opened up new paths for the future. Another and later new mode of perception, Mahler's systematic exploitation of the 'vulgar', was clearly foreshadowed by it and has met, as one might expect, with a rather similar hostile reaction;

---

[1] Introduction to the Penguin Score, 1955, p. 7.

likewise his unique musicalization of irony, a quality for a long time which was considered to be outside the scope of music—a clear case, this, of a feeling becoming 'accessible to music' and the finding (or founding) of the new style to accompany, to express, its emergence.

I have mentioned so far—and my choice has really been quite haphazard—examples of the conquering of emotional territories new to music which have met with persistent opposition. But there are many other examples, again widely contrasted in composer and category, where assimilation of the New has been swift. Berlioz's amazing and early plunge into the dream-life of the mind, for instance, in his *Symphonie fantastique*, which, these days, encounters little in the way of resistance though its impact remains as fresh as ever. Or many, perhaps too rarely considered, aspects of Tchaikovsky's genius—what one might call the functional hysteria which gives a work like *Francesca da Rimini* its peculiar character, or scenes in some of his operas, in *The Queen of Spades*, for example, where often the music seems able effectively to portray states of mind, e.g., a condition of hallucination, which hitherto have belonged rather to science (as subjects of study) than to art (as sources of inspiration). (Of course, once one starts on this particular tack examples are legion —think of the long line of succession which stems from Wagner's 'mad' Tristan in Act 3 of *Tristan und Isolde*: Strauss's *Salome* and *Elektra*, Berg's *Wozzeck*, and Britten's *Peter Grimes*, not to speak of Schoenberg's anonymous 'Frau' who is the sole *dramatis persona* in *Erwartung*.)

Perhaps it might be argued that some of my examples stand on the brink of the Unconscious. Stravinsky's *Le Sacre du printemps*, however, is well over the edge and dives deep down. Indeed, together with certain works by Schoenberg, *Le Sacre* brilliantly represents the exploring and exploitation of the Unconscious which, I have suggested, was a marked feature of the New (in all its spheres) in the early years of our century—though I hope I have sufficiently stressed the fact that precedents for this discovery exist throughout the arts and elsewhere, are part of the history of the human mind, that the New, in short, has always been accompanied by a manifest 'opening up of . . . new realms of feeling' (e.g., Beethoven's march in the ninth symphony's finale). It may be that it is only the degree, the scale, of the exploration which distinguishes Schoenberg's or Stravinsky's bold ventures from those of their predecessors. The principle is the same.

Le Sacre, in some respects, played the same rôle in Stravinsky's development as a composer as did the non-tonal period in Schoenberg's. It is true that the work may, perhaps, be regarded as the culmination of the 'Russian' ballets, as a natural consequence of trends already explicit in the *Firebird* and *Petroushka*, and thereby viewed at an angle that excludes Schoenberg, whose non-tonal works in a very real sense comprise a decisive break with his first period, despite the evolutionary links which hold fast across the dividing line. But what it is important to establish is not a superficial identity of achievement or coincidence of aims but the profoundly significant circumstance that both these masters of twentieth-century music, notwithstanding their (at this time) absolutely opposed creative methods and characters—on the contrary, the significance of the parallel is heightened *because* of the violent cleavage—each wrote works in the early years of the century (*Le Sacre*, 1911–12, the Five Pieces for Orchestra, 1909, or *Erwartung*, 1909) which introduced 'new modes of perception' and the new means of expressing them; each, moreover, uncovered a common source of inspiration—here, surely, we stumble on that unity of feeling, of aspiration, I mentioned earlier as characteristic of a 'period'?—in the Unconscious. [1] It is this kind of affinity,

---

[1] A recent conversation of Stravinky's (*Expositions*, pp. 140–8), suggests just how 'unconscious' was the composition of *Le Sacre*. He mentions the 'Danse sacrale', 'which I could play, but did not, at first, know how to write. . . . I was

45

I believe, which eventually will lend more of an appearance of homogeneity to the movements of art in our time than seems possible when, as now, we are too close to the events to see them in perspective. But that the twentieth century has its own, very consistent and, at length, demonstrable, pattern of development in the arts and related practices I have no doubt. It is my hope, in this book, tentative as its conclusions must be (not tentatively uttered, I confess, which makes for dull reading), to have made a few discriminations which will prove relevant to the total pattern as its shape emerges more and more clearly in the second half of the century.

How new *Le Sacre* sounded may be gauged from the reaction of its first audience who 'laughed, spat, hissed, imitated animal cries'. Some members, 'thrilled by what it considered a blasphemous attempt to destroy music as an art, and swept away with wrath, began very soon after the rise of the curtain to whistle, to make cat-calls, and to offer audible suggestions as to how the performance should proceed. . . . It was war over art.'[1] There were, of course, supporters of Stravinsky's 'new musical speech', as he himself describes it,[2] briefly and justly, as there were supporters of Schoenberg's 'new musical speech' in Vienna, the premières of whose music were often scandals as great as the première of *Le Sacre*. To the music of both composers written in these exciting years audiences responded with an immediacy of (predominantly hostile) emotion indicative of the musical impact the works themselves constituted. 'Impact', indeed, is not a bad word to use in connection with *Le Sacre*, for the work's early critics spoke

---

guided by no system whatever in *Le Sacre du printemps*. . . . I had only my ear to help me. I heard and wrote what I heard. I am the vessel through which *Le Sacre* passed.'

[1] Jean Cocteau and Carl Van Vechten quoted in Slonimsky, *op. cit.*, p. 138.

[2] *Conversations*, p. 46. I doubt if Stravinsky would so describe the works he wrote before *Le Sacre*. A small point, but an important one. At this distance in time, it is easy to overestimate *Le Sacre*'s derivations from the earlier ballets and to underestimate its stature as a monument of the New.

or wrote as if the music had done them personal injury, physical violence, as if the score of the ballet were an instrument of aggression. Paradoxical though it may seem, non-comprehension sometimes expresses itself in terms which are strikingly apt—they are wrong in their context because they are wrongly felt. But to sense *Le Sacre* as an act of aggression is by no means off the target. On the contrary it is very much on it. I would claim, in fact, that the new area of feeling which Stravinsky, in *Le Sacre*, made accessible to music, for which he was obliged to formulate a 'new musical speech', was Aggression, which I give a capital letter not out of pretentiousness but because I want to distinguish the powerful unconscious force plundered by Stravinsky from the aggression we meet in the dictionary.

There have doubtless been instances of functional aggression in music before Stravinsky (perhaps I may drop the capital now I have made my point?). Beethoven comes to mind, of course, as he always does when one is seeking out precedents for the New. But no composer apart from Stravinsky and no work, other than *Le Sacre*, has musicalized aggression in such depth on such a scale. Small wonder that the work was often experienced as a box on the ears. It still is, and rightly so. But now, diehards aside, and there are still a few about, we have learned to accept, to enjoy, the new experience Stravinsky offers us. We understand the 'new' speech because we have become reconciled to the feelings which promoted it. Strangely enough, the unique character of *Le Sacre*, which earned the work its baptism of scorn, was also guarantee of its relatively swift and more than superficial acceptance. After all, the indulgence of aggression affords a lavish degree of gratification—and in the guise of *Le Sacre* it may be relished without any guilty aftermath. Hence, in my view, the popular esteem this truly revolutionary score[1]

---

[1] In the case of *Le Sacre*, the ballet was the 'text' which provided the immediate means of comprehensibility in an otherwise new world of sound—compare my

enjoys today. It is no problem now to identify oneself with the work.

I think this question of 'identification' is important, and relevant, too, to our consideration of certain of Schoenberg's non-tonal works. It is not to be denied that *Erwartung*, say, or the Five Pieces for Orchestra have not made the headway which *Le Sacre* has. Is it not that the problem of 'identification' in—with—these works by Schoenberg is much more acute? Stravinsky, in so memorably utilizing the forces of aggression, was uncovering an area of feeling which, if the image will not be misunderstood, perhaps lay nearer the surface than many a level of feeling penetrated by Schoenberg: by which I do not mean to suggest for a moment that there is anything superficial about *Le Sacre* but, simply, that the musical experience it unfolds, though new, can be related without too great difficulty to mainsprings within the listener; however deeply sunk, they match up with the feelings released by Stravinsky. It seems to me, therefore, that *Le Sacre* may be said to have a genuine breadth of appeal; in fact, the history of the work's progress would suggest that such is the case. But Schoenberg? Here I feel I must return to my concept of the narrowness of some of the music from his non-tonal period. I do not doubt the musical genius of works like *Erwartung* or the Five Pieces for Orchestra (I think I have made that much clear); nor do I fail to appreciate the gift for submergence Schoenberg displays therein; nor, let me hasten to add, do I subscribe

---

remarks above (pp. 30–3) upon the function of the text in some of Schoenberg's innovating music. The seemingly objective and 'dramatic' justification of *Le Sacre*'s 'barbarity', i.e., the ballet's topic, 'Pictures of pagan Russia', is a characteristic example of the prop a composer often requires when launching out into the New. Those pagan Pictures, which seem so remote in the concert hall (indeed, to have faded out of sight and out of mind, while the music of *Le Sacre* remains so real), did their duty in enabling Stravinsky to compose his work secure in the knowledge that his adventurousness had a validating dramatic basis. Even a musical act of aggression needs, as it were, the legality behind it of a respectable motive. The 'crime' committed, legality may be thrown to the winds. *Le Sacre*, now, no longer needs its ballet!

for a moment to an assessment of these works in which 'morbid' figures prominently as an adjective. What troubles me is the exclusiveness, the narrowness, of the experience they offer. A vivid, exciting experience, the intensity of which is rarely met with in music from any period, a new experience, in truth; but the revelation seems to me to lack that breadth which I have pointed to as a feature of *Le Sacre*. Stravinsky, in that work, realizes in sound a world of feeling with which it is possible to identify oneself. Schoenberg, on the other hand, appears to me to demonstrate with consummate genius a private world, an *under*world (if I may remove the term for a moment from its normal context), which one may experience as an exotic glimpse of a great artist's inner life but with which it is difficult to establish personal contact, personal identification; and, when all is said and done, the possibility of that communion is what major art offers (what makes it major, surely?).

The final evaluation of a work like, say, *Erwartung* can never be a clear-cut affair. The piece is one of the major documents in the history of the New music and its importance on this count alone would guarantee it a celebrated future. But it is, of course, much more than that, a unique inspiration, a unique manifestation of Schoenberg's genius. These components, however, compelling as they are, do not add up to a great work of art. I think if we compare *Erwartung* with later masterpieces by Schoenberg, like *Moses und Aron* or that miraculous *opera buffa*, *Von Heute auf Morgen*, the limited experience the earlier work unfolds is clearly exposed against the rich perspectives offered by the later. Might I put it that we have here a contrast between 'closed' and 'open' worlds of experience? I would add, further, that the kind of major experience we encounter in Schoenberg's music, in his greatest works, in short, belongs to the period in his life when he had solved the problem of 'language'—the means of communication, in its profoundest sense; that, indeed, this kind of major experience was not a possibility in terms of the language Schoenberg discovered and developed during his non-tonal period, a period which I view, to an important degree, as one of necessary experiment and transition. (I must permit myself one qualification: that I am aware of the wide contrasts between works *within* the period 1907–16, that some works are more 'open' than others, e.g., *Pierrot lunaire.* But I shall let my generalization stand, based though it may be on the most extreme examples of what, to my ears, supports my point of view.)

May any conclusion be drawn from all this? I don't think it unfair to remark that Schoenberg himself did draw *his* conclusion from his own creative experience. He moved on, in truth, into a new—more 'open'!—world, after a protracted interlude devoted to consideration of musical organization and comprehensibility, to problems of language, in fact. I think Schoenberg himself realized that what he had achieved in his non-tonal compositions, as convincing a demonstration of his genius as the works themselves comprise, was not wholly adequate. It still did not divulge 'the principle capable of serving as a rule'. The 'rule' was to emerge in the works composed from 1920 onwards, after the period, if one may so describe it, of intensive creative meditation (1916–20).

I have suggested, then, that Schoenberg's historic plunge into the Unconscious raised, and, I believe, will continue to raise, real problems of understanding. It would seem that we must discriminate in art between unconscious forces which may be apprehended when musicalized and those which may not. Why certain composers' 'new modes of perception'—some of which I listed above—have proved swifter of acceptance than others may well be ascribed to the utility or otherwise of the mode concerned; and utility, in this context, I would judge by the accessibility *to* feeling of the feeling concerned. I don't see (feel) that Schoenberg's non-tonal works have an unclouded future in this respect. It cannot be simply a matter of

idiom, of a 'difficult' style. *Wozzeck*, as I have already
mentioned, was a child, by Berg, out of *Erwartung*. An
infant with somewhat diluted features, to be sure, more
given to compromise than its radical mother, but in very
many important stylistic respects—perhaps too many for
a completely healthy family situation—the spit image of
Mum. Yet despite this striking identity of language at one
level, *Wozzeck* commands a breadth of comprehension and
acclaim which I doubt will ever accrue to *Erwartung*. It is
not, to put it crudely, that *Wozzeck* is all that much easier
on the ear, but that the possibility of identification with
Berg's opera is so much the greater. (Needless to add,
Erwartung remains *Wozzeck*'s easy superior in invention
and inspiration; half-identification with *Erwartung*, for
me, offers a richer experience than total identification with
Wozzeck.)

We may concede, perhaps, that the peculiar nature of
Schoenberg's non-tonal music—some works more peculiar
than others—has hindered its progress. But the comments
I've made about it, whether right or wrong, are not those
which, in general, have been advanced by Schoenberg's
opponents as criticism of the non-tonal works, unless one
construes the frequent charge of 'morbidity' as a perverse
offspring of my own reservations, i.e., the misinterpreta-
tion of the depth and narrowness of Schoenberg's inspirations from this period as manifestations of 'the most
intense emotion, introspection and sordidity'[1] or 'neurasthenia and decadence'.[2]

[1] Iain Hamilton: 'Alban Berg and Anton Webern' in *European Music in the
Twentieth Century*, pp. 95–7. It is not easy to know at whom, exactly, Mr. Hamilton is directing his fusillade, but I think there can be no doubt that we may
assume Schoenberg to be among the targets since he refers broadly to 'the school
of Schoenberg' and the 'twelve-note school of composers' while adjusting his
sights. It is odd to note in passing to what distorted facts distorted feelings will
give rise. If we take Schoenberg alone, and allow Mr. Hamilton his distaste for
works like *Erwartung* and *Die glückliche Hand*, we are still left with *Moses und
Aron* and *Von Heute auf Morgen*, neither of which can easily be adjudged sordid or
[*contd. on next page*

[2] Constant Lambert: *Music Ho!*, London, 1934; Penguin Books, 1948, p. 38.

More Misconceptions

The behaviour of the charge, if I may so describe its history, follows familiar lines, familiar at least to students of Schoenberg's career. The verbal missiles become detached in time from the objects with which, however wrongly, they were associated—a genuine association, of a sort (which is not the same thing as a correct opinion or valid criticism)—but, instead of dying, like any other self-respecting organs when separated from their parent bodies, the misconceptions develop extraordinarily hardy and independent constitutions of their own and live on; one has met them again and again, our old friends neurasthenia and decadence, applied to works by Schoenberg from any period, of any character, with a truly astounding liberality, on the principle, one assumes, that what was good enough for *Erwartung* or *Pierrot* will still serve as handy ammunition, however much the context, the language—the music itself, in short—may have changed, so that there remains not even the dubious justification of wrong, but genuine—because then stimulated by contact with the music—association. But none of this need surprise us. I have written earlier of the detachment of the Method from the music, of the battle fought about the rights and wrongs of a means of composing, which waxed the fiercer the further the immensely protracted disputes drifted away from experience of the works from which the Method was evolved, when thought and feeling became hopelessly separated. Seen in this light, there is nothing novel about the thoughtless application of tattered and out-worn emotional labels to Schoenberg's music, a practice which

decadent. *Moses* musicalizes the Old Testament in a spirit that could hardly be loftier, and if Mr. Hamilton is dismayed by the sexual comedy of *Von Heute auf Morgen*, then he must regard *Figaro*, or—perhaps even more so—*Cosi*, as the *Lolita* of music. That Mr. Hamilton, moreover, happily writes of the 'twelve-note school' while it is obvious that he has in mind 'offending' works from Schoenberg's pre-serial period; that he strangely overlooks those strictly twelve-note works which must radically revise the principal burden of his argument—'There is little here of the direct expression of lofty, noble or heroic motives', etc.: these traits in his commentary support what I write of the confusion of issues which reigns in this field.

took no serious account of his development as a composer and failed to discriminate the steps which led to his achievements in the evolution of a language, of the 'principle capable of serving as a rule'.

The pattern is familiar. And if we are naive enough to be astonished at the continued obscuring of later events by the fog of misunderstanding from earlier (and quite different) days, how shall we survive a far more intense and significant paradox—one very relevant to any inquiry into the nature of Schoenberg's achievement—that the *pre*-serial works from the non-tonal period have often been condemned as characteristically grotesque and contrived examples of the Method? Perhaps there can be no clearer illustration than this, the inability or unwillingness to distinguish between serial and pre-serial music, of the intense degree of unreality which has so often pervaded discussion of Schoenberg's works; everything, indiscriminately, is disputed— and dismissed—in terms of the 'system', no matter whether or not the cap fits. Possibly rather more amusingly but no less revealingly—to be sure, another symptom—a work like Berg's *Wozzeck* is *praised* for showing so clearly what a composer, as distinct from a cerebral constructivist, an engineer, could do with the intractable 'system', how inspiration might mitigate mathematics; all this despite the fact that *Wozzeck* is as *pre*-serial as any non-tonal work by Schoenberg.

The one clear fact that emerges from the foregoing muddle is this: that a great deal of opposition was aroused by the very idea of the Method—indeed, by the idea of *a* method, a system.

One wonders how the tonal 'system'—quite correctly so called: it doesn't really require my quotation marks—with its complex grammar and myriad precepts, admonitions and prohibitions, has escaped criticism. Its rules are legion; its 'uniformity' has imposed a consistency of behaviour and integration of style upon composers howsoever diverse in character and wheresoever placed in chronology during the three hundred years or so that tonality has reigned as the sovereign rule in Western music. Composers have, throughout its history, challenged its authority, re-interpreted it, qualified, modified, defied, denied, re-asserted it. Tonality, none the less, remained enthroned, until toppled from its eminence by the convulsions which shook music towards the end of the nineteenth century. We show a preposterous misconception of the nature of the art of music if we imagine that this rule of (tonal) law was not sustained by the practice of a formidable discipline which each generation of composers has had consciously to apprehend, commit to memory and put to use like any other set of comparable data. The composer, in this sense, has never been 'free'. (Perhaps the only composer who was, was Schoenberg himself, in certain works from those crucial non-tonal, pre-serial years about which I have written above. He saw the necessity to surrender his free-dom: hence the creative development of the Method. It is typical of the scope of this amazing man's career that it should embrace both the peak of untrammelled freedom and the foundation of a new means of order. Typical, too, that those who were loudest in their defence of the artist's sacred 'freedom' were among the first to misrepresent Schoenberg's genuinely free compositions as characteristic specimens of the crippling 'system'!)

Familiarity, we are told, breeds contempt. Almost as bad, it breeds forgetfulness. Ears, across the centuries, had become so accustomed to the operation of the tonal system that it ceased to be recognized as a system. Musicians, of course, who had to go on learning it, to mas-ter an increasingly elaborate syntax, were not likely to suffer from this form of amnesia. But critics and listeners tended only to think in terms of an artist's freedom, neglecting the existence of the discipline which made free-dom a possibility (after all, freedom is a relative thing, not an absolute; moreover, without a language we can't enjoy 'free speech', neither in art nor society). And if familiarity

with tonality was one reason why the recognition of it as a
defined system of organization declined, another, surely,
rested in the development of a society, increasingly
mechanized, increasingly industrialized, increasingly *systematized*, in which the artist became more and more a
figure who represented an ideal 'freedom' denied to the
majority of the community? There was social pressure,
then, contributing to the phenomenon of the *isolated*
artist, so familiar a part of the cultural picture of modern
society, not only the pressure, generally acknowledged, of
neglect or indifference, though undoubtedly this too has
had a rôle to play in the widening divorce of artist and
public.

I wonder, sometimes, if the function of the artist, in
modern society, as scapegoat—i.e., the non-conformist who
must be punished or scorned for his dissent—has been
sufficiently studied? We create the artist in a shape that
we may either cherish or despise, love or hate, as the
inspired odd man out or dangerous anarchist; we need
him in both guises, as valuable symbol of freedom and
convenient example of the peril of non-conformity (to be
made an example of); and whether or no a social attitude
to the artist represents an accurate account of the artist's
function, is not strictly relevant in this context, where
what matters is *how* the artist is regarded socially. But for
the artist, neither the rôle of the esteemed rebel nor the
rôle of scapegoat is a particularly fruitful one. In previous
centuries one may be sure that the artist would not have
welcomed having freedom, as it were, thrust upon him.
On the contrary one might view him in earlier days as the
purveyor of order in a free society (and who can deny the
freedom that order bestows? Is this not a principle inherent in great art?). In our captive society, however, the
situation of the artist is very different. Can it be seriously
contested that in our own time, whether a 'myth' or not,
the concept of the 'free' artist has substantially influenced
artistic practice? At the very moment of writing, the

prevalence of action-painting, of tachisme, would seem to confirm that the myth can exert a very real influence. ('Current social values may, as Koestler has remarked, be extraneous to aesthetic merit, but they cannot be isolated from it.'[1])

The myth, of course, has not been the creation of our century alone. On the contrary, it was strong indeed in the nineteenth century, where many an artistic genius of the front rank acted out, in life, his rôle as transcender of established law and custom, as stubborn opponent of the mores of society. By the close of the nineteenth century the 'freedom' of the artist was proverbial, as was its corollary —widespread distrust and disapproval of the freedom which he exercised, to the bafflement and downright indignation of his audience.

I think it may be readily appreciated that Schoenberg, in rebuilding the basis of a language, was faced with an acutely paradoxical state of affairs. One might have thought that his unfolding of the Method would have silenced, or at least interested, those who complained loudest of the growing anarchy of music's language in the twentieth century. (After all, as I have suggested above, Schoenberg himself had found 'freedom' wanting and thus had concentrated upon creating, through his music, a new means of organization.) But the reception of the Method, as we have seen, was not at all of this perceptive order; and when we have allowed for the 'musical' reasons which promoted its dismissal, some of which I have already outlined, we still have to face the fact of yet another important source of hostility, in this case the socially derived but critically supported contention that Schoenberg's Method was tampering with that holy of holies, the artist's freedom. Here, indeed, one might say that the Method ran into headlong collision with the Myth; and there is no doubt that for many years Schoenberg's music was

---

[1] Quoted by Sir Hugh Casson in 'Beauty and the Beast', the *Observer*, March 1st, 1959, p. 11.

battered from—or rather by—both sides of the concept of untrammelled freedom: it was heard as anarchy on the one side, on the other as a most monstrous and unnatural systematization—not a promising context for the comprehension of Schoenberg's intentions as an artist.

I do not believe it can be denied that the social pressure I describe, *against* which Schoenberg was obliged to struggle when the secret of the Method was out, made a powerful contribution to the hindrance of understanding of his later and most mature music. This idea of freedom, which his Method seemed to undermine, had grown deep roots, especially among critics. It is not, perhaps, altogether without significance that the practice of criticism itself had immeasurably increased in extent and importance during the very period when the artist was developing his unwonted freedom (in an integrated culture the critic is superfluous). Indeed, one might say that critics have a vested interest in the artist's freedom—because if everything is possible for the artist, so too is everything possible for the critic; the critic's right of free speech, of free opinion, is scarcely less sacrosanct than the artist's, in fact, and scarcely less of a myth: criticism, like art, should be a discipline, not a nursery-like free-for-all where every opinion has a 'right' to be taken seriously. It is only in a time like ours when a devil's bargain has been struck between the free artist and the free critic that a phrase like 'it's all a matter of opinion' can bear so conclusive an interpretation, wear so convincing an air of finality. The assumption of anarchy as a prerogative of the artist has had disastrous consequences, not only in the sphere of creativity.

There were, then, very widely contrasted reasons why, until quite recently, Schoenberg's music has been only slowly accepted. As we have seen, there were not only genuine difficulties of comprehensibility at the aural level but also many other motives, perhaps extraneous to the music but no less real for that, which powerfully weighed against its progress, among them social factors, such as the dread of uniformity in an already too uniform society for which the inflation of the artist into a figure of unreal, even undesired, freedom takes on the guise of a compensatory fantasy. Does not this dread of uniformity boil down to standardized man's fear of stopping up the escape-valve which the artist represents, of standardization in a field where he has been taught only 'freedom' reigns? But some degree of standardization, of systematization, is an integral part of art. Let us remind ourselves of Le Corbusier's definition of standardization, the words which in many respects have comprised the text for this first chapter: standardization—'to obtain the status of a rule: to uncover the principle capable of serving as a rule'. And though Walter Gropius was writing specifically of the 'language' of architecture and industrial design we can approve his apt comments on this problem of uniformity:

Standardization is not an impediment to the development of civilization, but, on the contrary one of its immediate prerequisites.

The fear that individuality will be crushed out by the growing 'tyranny' of standardization is the sort of myth which cannot sustain the briefest examination. In all great epochs of history the existence of standards—that is the conscious adoption of type-forms—has been the criterion of a polite and well-ordered society; for it is a commonplace that repetition of the same things for the same purposes exercises a settling and civilizing influence on men's minds.[1]

Art, of course, is concerned with other things besides settling men's minds—the artist, indeed, often wants to *un*settle those whom he addresses. ('Art disturbs: Science reassures', as Braque has expressed it.) But a language, the existence of type-forms, will enable him to keep in touch with his audience, to remain comprehensible, even where he bursts out with the New. By the end of the nineteenth century the governing principle of tonality, which had created and served a language of music of wonderful rich-

[1] Walter Gropius: *The New Architecture and the Bauhaus*, London, 1935, pp. 34, 37.

ness, had become so weakened that it could no longer divulge the new vocabulary which was required to match the new images of composers like Schoenberg and Stravinsky. The resources of tonality were exhausted. Schoenberg made a heroic effort during his non-tonal, pre-serial period to make 'freedom' work, but failed, brilliant and influential though his failures were. Out of that extraordinary period of creative turbulence, truly a cauldron in which the future of the New music was on the boil, emerged the serial method, the principle which, as time has shown, proved capable of serving a large body of composers as a rule. The world-spread dissemination of the Method, indeed, which was so notable a feature of the musical scene after the end of the second world war, scarcely seemed to bear out a notorious and busily humorous prediction of Hindemith's, who wrote, in 1951:

Movements of this kind spring up like epidemics of measles, and they disappear just as enigmatically. We have already once seen a twelve-tone movement die, due to lack of interest on the part of musicians who liked music more than operations on music. That was shortly after World War I. At that time the germ was introduced to this country [the U.S.A.] and caused minor disturbances, which by now have all but disappeared, with a few scars remaining. After World War II, Europe was again infected, but already the patients are feeling better and there is hope that after some minor relapses only a few diehards will survive to be the prophets who, in quiet solitude, will prepare the next big outburst.[1]

One may contrast this with the words of another composer, Stravinsky, writing in 1957:

Nothing is likely about masterpieces, least of all whether there will be any. Nevertheless, a masterpiece is more likely to happen to the composer with the most highly developed language. This language is serial at present and though our contemporary development of it could be tangential to an evolution we do not yet see, for us this doesn't matter. Its resources have enlarged the present language and changed our perspective in it. Developments in language are not

---

[1] Paul Hindemith: *A Composer's World*, Harvard University Press, 1952, pp. 123–4.

easily abandoned, and the composer who fails to take account of them may lose the mainstream. Masterpieces aside, it seems to me the new music will be serial.[1]

Yet another opinion, again in marked opposition to Hindemith's, comes from Professor P. H. Lang, who observed, in 1958:

Schoenberg's innovation is the greatest single event in the music of the first half of our century, and though it has the earmarks of a transitional phenomenon, it is quite possible that the second half will be dominated by it. As an individual artistic feat it is very nearly unparalleled, and as it became generally known few musicians could remain untouched by it. We can observe every day how among our own American composers some of the best . . . are turning to it at the height of their well-formed, pronouncedly individual, and successful careers. Thus Schoenberg is more than a unique eruptive phenomenon; he dislocated music from all its strata, and with his appearance a new geological formation took place.[2]

Schoenberg nowhere claimed, at least publicly, that the aim of the Method was no less than *to rehabilitate the language of music in our century*. But when one assesses the consequences of the Method, the extent of its influence, it is hard not to credit it with this ambition. On reading Lang or Stravinsky, one might well conclude that the aim was, in fact, brought to a successful completion. Only a few years ago, indeed, it seemed as if the serial principle might govern music as tonality had in the past, permitting as many developments, departures and individual styles, while retaining, like tonality, sufficient common practice between individual composers and even between distinct historical periods to make 'serial' an adjective meaningful when applied to the half-century or the solitary composer; as versatile an adjective, in fact, as 'tonal'. The extraordinary turn of the historical wheel that brought Stravinsky into direct relation to Schoenberg—his adoption of the Method (see Chapter III, pp. 116–22)—only seemed

---

[1] *Conversations*, p. 131.

[2] Paul Henry Lang, in the *Musical Quarterly*, New York, Vol. XLIV, No. 4, October, 1958, pp. 507–8.

to consolidate, in the most dramatic way possible, the far-reaching effects of Schoenberg's re-establishment of a language for music. One might have been forgiven for assuming that a 'new geological formation' had taken place.

But a well-ordered serial universe was not to be. If events have confounded Hindemith's prediction, they have not confirmed Stravinsky's, either. The Newest music (if the term may be pardoned) of the later 'fifties and early 'sixties, which is, in part, the subject-matter of my Postcript (pp. 123–33), speaks a 'language' (one is obliged to use quotation marks) which has remarkably little to do with any of the linguistic developments of the first half of the century. To be sure, Webern, Stravinsky (of *Le Sacre*, especially) and late Debussy were the points of departure for the most radical composers of the new generation. But one becomes increasingly aware of the departures and less conscious of the points—the links with the past—as the Newest music grows older.

The situation in which we find ourselves in 1962 I discuss, briefly, in my Postcript. If Professor Lang were writing now, and not in 1958, one wonders if he would still commit himself to the opinion that Schoenberg's innovation might dominate the second half of the century? It is understandable enough, of course, that our attention should be almost wholly absorbed by the extremest manifestations of the Newest music. As a result, we tend perhaps to underestimate the persistence of the Method at less exotic levels of composition (one does not, naturally, forget Stravinsky's continuing adherence to the technique). Predictions, as we have seen, are always a risky business. But let me venture another: if, in the years to come, we are obliged to write about—to listen to—'music', not music, then we may be fairly confident that its 'language' will not be serial in the sense of the term that has been used in this book. But should the concept of music prevail, then I think one may hope that Stravinsky's prophecy may still be fulfilled. One cannot predict the shape of masterpieces to come (Britten!), but, 'Masterpieces aside, it seems to me the new music will be serial'.

II

CROSS-CURRENTS WITH CUBISM

If one were asked to sum up the greatest achievement of the New in a short phrase, I think 'the successful creation of a new language' would serve as adequate response. It is significant that both the major musical geniuses of the twentieth century, Schoenberg and Stravinsky, were obliged to abandon the styles of which, as younger men, they were undoubted masters—in neither case could a 'bygone aesthetic' serve as a vehicle of the New; and if we turn to painting we see there, too, that the artist comparable in so many ways with Schoenberg and Stravinsky, Picasso, found himself compelled to abandon his early manner. Like the composers, the painter had to relinquish the language he used so masterfully in his Blue and Rose periods and create, out of his painting, out of his inner artistic experience, the new means which would match his 'new mode of perception'. Is there a more convincing example than Cubism, the movement with which Picasso was so profoundly involved, of the relation between new ways of feeling and new means of expression which has so often been mentioned in these pages?[1] One might say that it was a feature of the great founders of the New in art that their careers, without exception, embraced a powerful turning against, away from, their early styles. Every

---

[1] Some early and very stimulating thoughts on the relation between music and painting in the twentieth century are to be found in Eric Walter White's *Stravinsky's Sacrifice to Apollo*, London, 1930, pp. 77–85.

artist, of course, develops away from the models which he must imitate in his youth, but the kind of mature renunciation of early influences we meet in artists like, say, Beethoven or Wagner, has nothing in common with the sharpness of the reaction against their early styles we encounter in Schoenberg or Stravinsky, where we can properly speak of a division between the Old and the New, not a gradual evolution from an immature style to a mature one purged of eclectic impurities. In Schoenberg or Picasso there is a radical break between how they began and how they went on.

I do not think this is the place to argue all over again the *need* for the New. Hundreds of thousands of words have been written about the predicament of musicians at the turn of the century, who were left with a worn-out language as a legacy. The fact of this debility, one may agree, has been established; more than that, I think one may say it has been received. In any event, what better evidence is there of the need for the New than the existence of the New itself? It is from that position that I set out.

The words of the Belgian painter and architect, Henry van de Velde, precisely convey the essence of the end-of-the-century situation and, at the same time, emphasize an important element in the act of the artists who cut loose from the past:

The real forms of things were covered over. In this period the revolt against the falsification of forms and against the past was a moral revolt.[1]

Both Schoenberg and Stravinsky have been termed revolutionaries, mostly with abusive intent; both have stoutly denied any such allegiance. Stravinsky has said:

. . . I am completely insensitive to the prestige of revolution. All the noise it may make will not call forth the slightest echo in me. For revolution is one thing, innovation another.[2]

---

[1] Giedion, *op. cit.*, pp. 291–2.
[2] Stravinsky: *Poetics of Music*, Harvard University Press, 1947, p. 13.

Revolution and Innovation

Schoenberg, likewise, scarcely speaks with the tongue of an incendiary:

One of the safest methods of acquiring attention is to do something which differs from the usual, and few artists have the stamina to escape this temptation. I must confess that I belonged to those who did not care much about originality. I used to say: 'I always attempted to produce something quite conventional, but I failed, and it always, against my will, became something unusual!'[1]

One of Stravinsky's sentences deserves italicizing, so concisely does it distinguish between revolution and innovation, between destruction and new building: *For revolution is one thing, innovation another*. And there is a sentence of Schoenberg's about the Method which clearly stresses the positive spirit in which his innovation was conceived: *The method of composing with twelve tones grew out of a necessity*.[2] Something *grew*. Nothing was destroyed.

Van de Velde, whom I have quoted above—an extraordinary man who designed his own house and its contents rather than live the 'lie' that architecture and furniture and interior decoration had become at the end of the nineteenth century—sensitively underlines the morality of the modern movement in the arts, the moral assertion which the New represented. This was not a movement of iconoclasts (it was the minor tributaries, long since dried up, who thought all would be carried before them on a wave of brutal reaction against the past; the noise they made was in inverse proportion to their artistic significance). On the contrary, Schoenberg, as his words suggest, was almost an innovator unwilling and surprised; and Stravinsky's exceptional feelings about the past, about the musical past, are notorious—indeed, they are intimately bound up with the actual process of his creativity. As Stravinsky himself puts it with admirable objectivity, when composing, when seeking out his musical material, his 'building material', for a new work, he sometimes plays

---

[1] Schoenberg, *op. cit.*, p. 181.   [2] Ibid., p. 103.

the 'old masters', 'to put myself in motion'; and very
often, as we know, whichever old master has set the
Stravinsky motor ticking over, leaves his imprint behind
him. But Stravinsky and the past is a whole subject in
itself and must await a later page. For the moment it is
enough if we recognize that both he and Schoenberg, each
in their different—almost opposite—ways, were engaged
not in demolition but in construction.

The morality of their stand *against* the past rested in
their realization that the language into which they were
born no longer held 'true'; and indeed, if we survey the
musical scene at the end of the nineteenth century and the
beginning of the twentieth, we may be astonished to discover how many talents, even quite substantial talents,
still hopefully and even authoritatively created in styles
and forms that seemed to have life only because life had so
long inhabited them. One cannot blame the artists themselves for failing to diagnose death while the patient yet
appeared to breathe. There is less reason or excuse for the
historian or critic to indulge in faulty judgment; but in
these spheres too it is all too easily possible, on the basis of
a very real discrimination of the values of the past, of a
respect for the tradition of competence and craftsmanship
which the past represents, to discern artistic significance
in stubbornly conservative works written in a period of the
emerging New, despite their linguistic anachronism and, in
a very strict sense, their lack of a future. To reject a work
of this kind, which may well seem to be beautiful in the
old style, can be a painful experience for the critic, conscious as he is of the past. But he must, in his own small
way, make his stand, and say No to the lie that is implicit
in the use, however masterful, of a language which has lost
the power of meaningful speech. One must say No to
Richard Strauss's *Alpensinfonie*, for instance, on this
ground alone, and to many another of his works, even the
better ones, where a similar air of complete unreality per-
vades his grandiose rhetoric. (I sometimes think that of

Strauss's music only *Salome* and *Elektra* among the operas, and a few of the early orchestral works, will survive.) One must say No, much more reluctantly, to composers like Hans Pfitzner and Franz Schmidt, composers of greater integrity than Strauss perhaps, which makes their rejection all the harder, all the more painful. No moral blame attaches to these honourable musicians; but their music, notwithstanding, can not, must not, be taken seriously. It represents only too acutely a kind of insidious expertness which has the manner of genius but none of its substance. Transitional periods are almost bound to throw up these rather tragic figures, good men and fine musicians, who seem compelled by some ironic destiny to create in a style that is already an illusion. They are plainly victims of Time, and their gifts—sufficient to enable them to play their rôles with conviction but not enough to rescue them from their fate—only intensify their predicament. Their status could be more easily assessed if they were plainly incompetent composers—which they are not. On the contrary, it is their superior talents which confuse the aesthetic issue.

The critic, as I have suggested, may well find himself faced with painful decisions to be made. After all, he himself can also be a victim of Time, and there is no doubt to my mind that those of us born in or shortly after a particularly eventful period of radical change, however perceptive we may be of the New, are liable to hear in these pendants to the immediate past an authenticity which is, in fact, a projection, on to the merely imitative and second-hand, of our training and environment; we are, so to say, conditioned by the past to react favourably to certain type-forms and formulae even when they are no longer charged with inspiration or invention. It is right that we should be suspicious of many manifestations of the New, especially the fashionable New, because there are, of course, as many masks and masquerades in this sphere as there are faked Old Masters clinging on from the past.

Fashion hunting is not a particularly fruitful sport, though it has its practitioners among the critics (not to speak of composers). On the other hand, exaggerated esteem for competence, for traditional virtue, is not one whit to be preferred; bad, that is, *dead*, music is no better, no livelier, for being decently composed. In some ways this overestimation of competence can be even more damaging than a reckless greeting of the latest fashion as promise of a new dawn. However that may be, I have no doubt that the problem constituted by the merits of these marginal figures, these Old Conservatives as one might describe them, will simply vanish of its own accord, along with the memory of their music. A few generations more may see the establishment of ears that can discriminate more clearly than we can in this still-transitional epoch between a 'classical' language which lives and the dead language which is not and cannot be 'classical' because it has never been alive.

My position is perfectly straightforward. I shall continue to enjoy a work like, say, Pfitzner's *Palestrina*, because I know, when next I hear it, I shall feel something positive about it. But I believe most of that feeling to be a reflex action. I can no longer regard my response as a proper instrument of criticism, to be exercised in the work's favour. It must be faced that one's feelings can betray one, and there is a wide area of potential treachery in just this category of creative figure.[1]

Does this apply to the early periods of the masters of the New who, almost without exception, started their creative careers in the old style? In a sense, the composers themselves are their best and severest critics. The abandonment of the 'bygone aesthetic' makes its own comment, whether we think of Stravinsky and his early Russian ballets, of Schoenberg and his *Verklärte Nacht* or *Gurrelieder*, or of Bartók and his early orchestral suites, for instance. The

---

[1] We should be better employed, I feel, listening to Charles Ives than to Pfitzner. The more one hears of Ives, indeed, the more central and anticipatory appears to be his relationship to the first half of the twentieth century.

degree of abandonment, its intensity so to say, depends largely upon the scale of what has to be abandoned. In this respect both Stravinsky and Bartók were more fortunate than Schoenberg, who in his early music was heir to a very great tradition indeed, though a defunct one; its exhaustion, of course, comprised its crippling burden. Schoenberg, then, had more to be rid of than his great contemporaries. The act of rejection was a heroic one and we must continually remind ourselves of the courage he showed in making the break. As Professor Lang rightly observes, 'Schoenberg and his school represent the first real breaking away from the legacy of the long nineteenth century.'[1] We may say that the radical nature of the breaking away was conditioned by the very size of the historic European tradition out of which Schoenberg was born. At the same time, there is a complementary aspect to the breaking away; one doubts, that is, if Schoenberg could have re-created a language for music in the twentieth century had he *not* been born out of the great tradition which he had to abandon. (His achievement of a language, of course, all else apart, guarantees him his place in the history of music.) It is not reasonable, I think, to be surprised that Schoenberg himself, despite the example of his mature music, the standards it set, of which he must have been aware, did not 'disown' his earlier style; as he said himself, in a famous phrase, 'I do not know which of my compositions are better; I like them all, because I liked them when I wrote them.'[2] This, of course, is a perfectly valid statement from Schoenberg's point of view, but the obligation to 'like' is not incumbent upon us as it was upon the composer. (Stravinsky, by the way, is more critical of his early works. I think he may now like some of them less than he did when he wrote them.) The kind of mastery Schoenberg reveals in his early works is exceptional, and so is the intensity with which the invention is

---

[1] Lang, *op. cit.*, p. 503.　　　　　[2] Schoenberg, *op. cit.*, p. 213.

felt, an intensity which is almost a feature in itself of his art, of his personality; it is no less present in the later works than in the earlier, perhaps sometimes disturbingly so; how grateful one can be for Stravinsky's profound capacity for repose after exposure to a bout of Schoenberg's brilliant nerves! (It is odd how these great figures complement one another at almost every turn: what a relief to encounter Schoenberg's boundless feeling after subjection to Stravinsky's restraints and abstentions!) Only after a few of Schoenberg's finest works can one echo a great phrase of Van Gogh's who, in a letter to his brother, Theo, wrote of 'some canvases, which will retain their calm even in the catastrophe'; and Mr. W. H. Auden is almost right in suggesting that 'what we mean when we speak of a work of art as "great" has, surely, never been better defined than by the concluding relative clause' of the quotation.[1] One can think, however, of certain works of art which are not 'calm', which, on the contrary, seem to possess a sense of impending catastrophe (like some of Schoenberg's own) and yet, one may be sure, will survive the catastrophe itself. 'Calm', in short, is not a final criterion of judgment; but there is no doubt that very many of the greatest works of art possess it, and among musicians of the twentieth century Stravinsky seems to have a capacity for calm which makes Van Gogh's words peculiarly relevant to his case.

Of course, Schoenberg's music may grow calmer as one understands it better; one must be wary of reading into it a turbulence which may, in fact, be no more than the register of the impact his music has made on one's own feelings. In any event, what I sometimes react against in the music of his maturity is an intensity of feeling which can become disproportionate, disruptive of the total shape and poise of a work. But in this later period there is certainly no lack of a language sufficiently vital and developed

---

[1] W. H. Auden: 'Calm Even in the Catastrophe', a review of the letters of Van Gogh, in *Encounter*, April, 1959, pp. 37–40.

to carry the weight of emotion. Such is not always the case, to my ears, in the earlier works where there is, on occasion, a discrepancy between the significance of the feeling and the significance of the invention expressing it. An example is the theme of the Adagio from the first *Kammersymphonie* (1906), a theme Schoenberg quotes in his essay 'Heart and Brain in Music' in *Style and Idea*.[1] The melody is marked *sehr ausdrucksvoll* and its expressive intention is beyond doubt (as, of course, is its sincerity); none the less, I feel a distinct gap between the expressive intention and the expressive achievement of this passage, the intensive chromaticism of which, while accurately recording the composer's ardent emotion like a graph, only imperfectly conveys the experience which he wishes to share as sound. However vivid the feeling, however powerful the emotion, when the language is tired, as it is here, the result can only be largely negative. Indeed, of the historical stage when this work was written, I think one can say, paradoxical though it may seem, that it was no longer possible significantly to express feeling in terms of chromatic textures, although, in fact, the language of concentrated chromaticism was *still* the language of 'feeling'; but only in the sense that the style was inherited from the past, where its association with feeling had, of course, been a living one. No new expressive language had yet been formulated, hence even Schoenberg, in a work that often strikingly prophesies his future development and the future of modern music (the New, indeed, is to be heard in that famous sequence of ascending fourths which comprises the *Kammersymphonie*'s motto) was obliged to make a chromatic gesture when in *sehr ausdrucksvoll* mood, despite the fact that the language of chromaticism was moribund, had become a petrified symbol of feeling, a statement, 'here I feel, and here', composed in a language of symbols and images and gestures of feeling which were no longer

---

[1] Schoenberg, *op. cit.*, pp. 164–5.

valid. But after all, what alternative was there? A new approach to tonality, for Schoenberg, was not possible, at least not at that time (his new approach came, but much later). There was no language of feeling available other than that of the bankrupt past, for which reason Schoenberg, to whom imperfect feeling in music must have been anathema, was increasingly stimulated to develop a new language (there are plenty of signs, for that matter, of his searching mind in the often very fresh and novel manner in which he handles chromaticism; but this sort of new look, even when it is Schoenberg's, is not really more than face-lifting of a very superior kind: it does not represent the radical re-thinking which the situation required).

Schoenberg's sentence I have quoted above, 'I do not know which of my compositions are better', etc., suggests an equality of significance for his works, irrespective of their style. 'I like them all, because I liked them when I wrote them.' But we, who didn't father them, are spared the necessity of having parental feelings about them. On the contrary, we must discriminate. Schoenberg himself had to discriminate, after all, and discriminate *against* his early style, however he may afterwards have cared to phrase his attitude to his work as a whole. The serial works, the necessity for the unfolding of the Method, do in themselves constitute, as I have said, a criticism of the early works, a recognition of their imperfections and limitations. We scarcely need reminding how painful Schoenberg found it to abandon an aesthetic of which he was master, for which he had the profoundest respect—more than that, reverence. We know from the tonal works he continued to write even at the height of his maturity, when the Method was long established, how strong the yearning was to turn back to the old style. He said himself:

... I was not destined to continue in the manner of *Transfigured Night* or *Gurrelieder* or even *Pelléas and Mélisande*. The Supreme Commander had ordered me on a harder road.

But a longing to return to the older style was always vigorous in me; and from time to time I had to yield to that urge.[1]

And he continues: 'This is how and why I sometimes write tonal music. To me stylistic differences of this nature are not of special importance.' He concludes with the sentence which has provided the text for these last pages.

All this, of course, is a typical artist's attitude. A critical or historical assessment must be shaped quite otherwise. One cannot say simply that the difference between *Verklärte Nacht* and the Variations for Orchestra is a 'stylistic difference'. The major experience offered by the latter was not possible in the linguistic terms of the former. This, indeed, is a matter of *language*, not of style; and it is the quality of the language which facilitates the experience of the Variations, which limits the experience of *Verklärte Nacht*. Of course, Schoenberg's early music will live on, because his majestic later development can never fail to arouse curiosity about his origins. But again I feel that future generations, born out of reach of our immediate past, will be less and less interested in those origins as music, though they must always retain significance as documents of the emerging New. In any event, we must realize that the *Gurrelieder* are not of the same importance as the string trio; and I have little doubt that ears perhaps still to be conceived will come to this conclusion without any of the elements of pain that are likely to be part of discriminatory judgments made by us. I have already suggested that our present historical situation is confusing because we live in a period of transition, when our emotional entanglement with the past tends to corrupt our insight. It is especially difficult—painful—to assert a discrimination in the face of early works such as Schoenberg's, which so masterfully exploit the old style. But it would be doing his genius a serious disservice if one did not have it clear in one's mind that his stature as a

---

[1] Schoenberg, *op. cit.*, pp. 212–13.

major artist depends upon the music of his maturity, when he was able to dispose a language which was a match for the quality and character of his experience.

The development of a new language in music has its parallel in the other arts. It is possible, perhaps, to discern a pattern, faint and fragmentary though it may appear at this premature stage of excavation, which seems to lend to at least some of the most important arts a common background. What may be, possibly, only a segment of the pattern—but a highly interesting one—is the preoccupation of so much of the New, whether architecture, literature, painting, or music, with Time. Time, in fact, has swept into the foreground of twentieth-century art. Think of Joyce's *Ulysses*, of Proust's *Remembrance of Things Past*, in which quite new concepts of timeless Time are introduced into a literary form which had been a veritable bastion of narrative or chronological time. The study of architecture by Sigfried Giedion, from which I have quoted so often with admiration, is significantly entitled *Space, Time and Architecture*, and one of the most stimulating parallels he draws is between the New in architecture and the New in painting; or, more exactly, he uncovers the common background—the 'research into space' —which lent both Cubism and the modern movement in architecture a remarkable similarity of face. We may speak here, without exaggeration, of a language common to both paintings and buildings; and the common pattern derives from a common preoccupation, the interpenetration of space and time. Giedion describes Cubism thus:

It views objects relatively: that is, from several points of view, no one of which has exclusive authority. And in so dissecting objects it sees them simultaneously from all sides—from above and below, from inside and outside. It goes around and into its objects. Thus, to the three dimensions of the Renaissance which have held good as constituent facts throughout so many centuries, there is added a fourth one—time.[1]

---

[1] Giedion, *op. cit.*, p. 432.

'The presentation of objects from several points of view', he continues, 'introduces a principle which is intimately bound up with modern life—simultaneity'; and that very principle is no less intimately bound up with much modern architecture, where we may comprehend inside and out-side—and many other hitherto hidden relations—simultaneously; an experience which, previously, was dependent upon chronological appraisal of isolated relations. Apprehension of the total relation between all the parts (or planes) could only be accomplished by a feat of mental reconstruction. A simple example of the kind of simultaneity Giedion has in mind is the combined profile and full face which we encounter in Picasso's portrait, *L'Arlésienne*, painted in the early years of the twentieth century. Another is Le Corbusier's astounding Villa Savoye (1929–31), which conveys a simultaneity of exterior and interior, of inner and outer space, with breathtaking virtuosity.

That this concept of space-time is, in fact, a persistent pattern in twentieth-century art, of whatever nature, would seem to be remarkably confirmed when we discover that Schoenberg, in his essay 'Composition with Twelve Tones', demonstrates what is unmistakably space-time in terms of music. He first expresses it thus:

THE TWO-OR-MORE DIMENSIONAL SPACE IN WHICH MUSICAL IDEAS ARE PRESENTED IS A UNIT. Though the elements of these ideas appear separate and independent to the eye and the ear, they reveal their true meaning only through their co-operation, even as no single word alone can express a thought without relation to other words. All that happens at any point of this musical space has more than a local effect. It functions not only in its own plane, but also in all other directions and planes, and is not without influence even at remote points. . . . A musical idea, accordingly, though consisting of melody, rhythm, and harmony, is neither the one nor the other alone, but all three together.[1]

There could be no clearer definition of 'simultaneity' in

---

[1] Schoenberg, *op. cit.*, p. 109.

music than Schoenberg's last sentence. Music indeed, one discovers, has long been a resident in space-time, longer than the arts of painting, literature or architecture. The possibility of simultaneity, in fact, has always been one of the riches denied the plastic or literary arts but possessed by music in full measure; and what Schoenberg describes (his italics) as '*the unity of musical space*', a space which demands '*an absolute and unitary perception*' and in which 'there is no absolute down, no right or left, forward or backward', is not, of course, confined to serial compositions, though I think it not altogether without significance that it was the founder of the serial method who formulated the equivalent of space-time in music so succinctly. For there is, without doubt, something peculiarly space-time-like about a serial construction. What Giedion wrote in 1927 about the houses of Mies van der Rohe and Le Corbusier, part of the Werkbund exhibition at Stuttgart, might well serve as an accurate description of serial composition: 'Here is continuous energy at work: nothing in our life remains an isolated experience; everything stands in a many-sided interrelationship—within, without, above, below!'[1] Serial technique, in fact, offers the strictest parallel to the 'many-sided interrelationship—within, without, above, below!' which Giedion discerns as so emphatic a characteristic of the New in architecture, and at the same time creates the ideal conditions for the realization of the intensest 'unity of musical space'. It is, after all, the basic set which comprises the total texture of serial music, which inevitably ensures that 'everything stands in a many-sided interrelationship—within, without, above, below!', which offers a combination of perspectives, a 'simultaneity' *par excellence*, and a new space-time relation—for I think the integration of serial music, the totality of it, does facilitate the unfolding of the musical idea in a combination of planes and relations ('within, without, above, below!'; or, if one wishes, one

---

[1] Giedion, *op. cit.*, p. 553; Schoenberg, *op. cit.*, p. 113.

may recall Schoenberg's words, which convey the same truth from the opposite angle of approach, 'no absolute down, no right or left, forward or backward') with an instantaneity which introduces a space-time scale new to music. It was this aspect of Schoenberg's Method which his pupil and disciple, Anton Webern, seized upon and developed as a leading principle in his art. The 'brevity' of Webern's compositions resides in his concentrated application of Schoenberg's innovation, one of the consequences of the 'research into space' which was a feature of the arts in the first decades of the twentieth century.

It seems to me, therefore, that to draw a parallel between Cubism and the New architecture, on the one hand, and Schoenberg's Method on the other, is to plot a genuine identity of pattern between the arts in a given period; and, in fact, the parallel between the developments of Cubism and serial technique runs more strictly than I may have suggested. For instance, can it be doubted that the abandonment of tonality in music is not matched in painting by the abandonment of perspective? So remarkable is the coincidence of principle in both these historic manifestations of the New that one might almost suspect collusion! And collusion, of a kind, is just what we encounter in this remarkable alignment of eruptive events in two of the major arts of the century, upheavals which occurred, amazingly enough, in the *same* years—1907–8. There could hardly be a clearer case than this of the 'common background' shared by artists.

I find it surprising that the wellnigh simultaneous birth of Picasso's *Les Demoiselles d'Avignon* and Schoenberg's second string quartet—precisely comparable creative gestures—has attracted so little attention; moreover, if one examines the development of Cubism in greater detail, an intriguing accumulation of correspondences with the evolution of the Method builds up. At the outset, we have in painting a period of crisis when the New, as it

were, hangs in the air, its proximity sensed, perhaps some
of its features already revealed, but its main outline still
wreathed in mystery. Giedion quotes a painter who par-
ticipated in the Cubist movement and said of its begin-
nings:

There was no invention. Still more, there could not be one. Soon it was
twitching in everybody's fingers. There was a presentiment of what
should come, and experiments were made. We avoided one another; a
discovery was on the point of being made, and each of us distrusted
his neighbours. We were standing at the end of a decadent epoch.[1]

Musical history divulges a somewhat similar situation.
We have seen already that the advent of the New was
to be discerned in men who were Schoenberg's and
Stravinsky's seniors, composers like Debussy or Mahler.
In painting, there was, of course, Cézanne, in whose work
one can feel the new language, the new mode of perception,
breaking through to the surface, in exactly the same way
as one senses the emerging New in Mahler's later symphonies or the music of Debussy's final phase.[2] (Cézanne
died in 1906—five years before Mahler, twelve years
before Debussy.)

We know, too, that the principles which Schoenberg
eventually formulated were, rather like the principles of
Cubism, 'twitching in everybody's fingers'. There is the
curious fact that Josef Hauer, the Austrian composer and
theorist, evolved a method, a twelve-note technique,
which, though very different from Schoenberg's and certainly less significant (because it did not really provide
the basis for a renovation of language, the need of his
time), was demonstrably part of the common background
out of which Schoenberg's Method finally stepped into the
foreground. Schoenberg himself praised Hauer's theories,
and in the early 1920s wrote to him in a letter that he
(Hauer) was searching for the same thing in the same way

---

[1] Giedion, *op. cit.*, p. 431.

[2] In architecture there was Charles Rennie Mackintosh and his momentous
Glasgow School of Art, built between 1897 and 1909.

as Schoenberg himself.[1] We are not obliged to examine the Hauer-Schoenberg relation in greater detail, for the only point that claims our attention here is the composers' labouring at a common objective, to quite an important degree in common harness, though one independently assumed.

These pregnant climates and atmospheres which portended the birth of the New surrounded both painting and music. It is interesting that Schoenberg, however, took much longer to achieve a final formulation of his language than did his contemporaries in the field of painting. What Mr. Roland Penrose calls the 'Heroic Days' of Cubism preceded the outbreak of the first world war. He writes later, 'Since the appearance of the *Demoiselles d'Avignon* [1907] the new style had had only seven years to evolve, but the pace of its development had been vertiginous. Its influence had spread in all directions. Even painters of established repute, such as Matisse, who could not endorse its discoveries, found themselves adopting certain of its principles, until it could be said that no artist sensitive to the problems of painting could escape being influenced to some degree. At the same time the storm of anger that cubism had aroused among academicians and Philistines was equally significant. No one in fact who professed an interest in the arts could ignore it.'[2]

All this sounds a very familiar note. We have encountered much the same situation in our survey of the reception the Method was given. Another striking parallel resides, I think, in the crystallization of the New, in both painting and music, about a single figure. Although both Cubism and the Method may have been hanging in the air, it was Picasso and Schoenberg who finally grasped at the imminent intangible and materialized it in art.[3]

---

[1] Schoenberg: *Briefe*, ed. Erwin Stein, Mainz, 1958, p. 107.

[2] Roland Penrose: *Picasso: His Life and Work*, London, 1958, p. 183.

[3] I am aware that the history of Cubism, of its origins especially, is extraordinarily confusing; that it was, above all, paintings by Braque, his *Estaque*

Picasso and Schoenberg

Picasso has often been mentioned in the same breath as Stravinsky, as if their creative characters had much in common. But it is, in fact, Schoenberg rather than Stravinsky who matches up more closely and meaningfully with the painter, at least with the heroic period of Picasso's artistic development, from the Blue and Rose periods to the great Cubist revolution of the first decades of the twentieth century; in later years, it would seem that Picasso has turned away from his committal to the radical language which he himself initiated and practised, to rely too readily upon the virtuosity of his technique and his unfailingly fertile impulse to make something out of everything and anything. One does feel that a certain lack of seriousness has overtaken this great genius, however much one may admire his spirit and invention, and often the beauty of both; he cannot, I think, wholly escape a charge of superb triviality. But this aside is incidental, or at most it suggests a striking contrast with the later development of Schoenberg who, though he might well have benefited from a draught of Picasso's capacity for joy in his 'making', kept plodding on until the end of his life, as absorbed in—

---

landscapes, which provoked Matisse to the coining of the very term itself, i.e., his dismissive judgment of the works as made up of 'little cubes'. These paintings, moreover, 'anticipate by almost a year those which Picasso was to paint in a similar vein at Horta de San Juan in 1909'. Thus writes John Richardson in his preface to *Braque* in the Penguin Modern Painters Series, 1959, p. 8. Perhaps, then, one should, as Mr Richardson does, refer to the movement as a 'joint venture'. (It is strange, indeed, that Cubism, like dodecaphony, should have had two parent figures, though Hauer, of course, has not proved to be a creator of Braque's significance.) On the other hand, I am with Mr. Penrose, when he writes in *Picasso*, p. 147, that the '*Demoiselles d'Avignon* in 1907 was in advance of any other creative achievement'. It was Braque's experience of this revolutionary canvas that shook him out of his Fauvism and into Cubism; thus it would seem to me that Picasso deserves his pre-eminent position. Of course, that Braque played so leading a rôle in the formation and development of Cubism—at one period both Braque and Picasso pooled their ideas and worked in unison (Richardson, p. 10) with the result that 'the authorship of their paintings at the height of the cubist period is often difficult to determine' (Penrose, p. 147)—is itself indicative of a state of affairs which we also encounter in the history of modern music: 'a community of ideas . . . ripening in an atmosphere alive to the urgent need for a new form of expression'. The parallel with the evolution of dodecaphony is very striking.

and by—his language in his final period as he was in his days of most acute questing. One may regret that a Mediterranean wit did not inform Schoenberg's Teutonic solemnity—'Let us show the world, if nothing else, that Music at least could not have advanced without the Austrians, while we know what the next step must be'[1]— but there is no denying that it is the earnest Schoenberg rather than the playful Picasso who offers late works of a grandeur and integrity that seem naturally to fulfil the promise of the heroic days of modern music. There is no abandonment of his hard-won position, no decline into triviality.

But though the later careers of Picasso and Schoenberg may diverge, in the earlier stages of their mutual explorations of new territory (which were not necessarily chronologically coincidental except for the astonishing common birth-years of the *Demoiselles d'Avignon* and the second string quartet) there are many instances where we see both major manifestations of the New sharing certain common characteristics. We find, for example, that many of Picasso's friends, like Schoenberg's when confronted with *his* new aesthetic, were bewildered by the 'revolution' implicit in the *Demoiselles* canvas; even Braque, who was soon to join Picasso in his great adventure, was at first a sceptic. The *Demoiselles*, moreover, was not exhibited, was not 'demonstrated'. For many years it remained in Picasso's studio and was not, in fact, put on public view 'until thirty years after it had been painted'. But as Mr. Penrose points out, 'even during the early days of its seclusion, the influence of the picture on those who saw it was profound'. It was Picasso's painter friends and colleagues, and of course Picasso himself, who took up the challenge of the *Demoiselles*, and developed the new language in succeeding acts of creation. There was no launching of a theory or a system, not even the limelight of a public furore. (The scandal was to come later.) First, there

---

[1] Schoenberg, *op. cit.*, p. 108.

was the impact of a distinctly new mode of perception on a group of creative minds. What followed was not theorizing, but paintings, in every sense deeds not words. 'Cubism . . . did not begin with theories. There was no question in Picasso's mind of creating a system any more than of founding a school.' 'Picasso had, already in 1908, a right to say he knew nothing and wanted to know nothing of Cubism. He playfully asserted that imitators did much better than inventors.' But, of course, theorizing did follow; as Mr. Penrose has it, 'Science inevitably arrives after the *fait accompli* to rationalize and elaborate the discoveries we owe to art.' Picasso and Braque may, as Mr. Richardson contends, have 'disdained picture-makers such as Gleizes, Metzinger, and the rest of the *Section d'Or*, who tried to make a formula out of Cubism'. But part of the strength of Cubism rests none the less in the fact that it did prove to represent a vocabulary which artists of whatever differences in character could employ as a means of expressive communication. The founders of Cubism were right to stress a purely creative and intuitive approach, just as it was right of Schoenberg to emphasize the creative evolution of the Method; but it would be ingenuous to pretend that part of the profound significance of both these developments of the New did not rest in the linguistic possibilities they opened up for the founders' contemporaries and successors. Cubism, as Sir Herbert Read remarks, illustrates 'a coherent theory of art'. It is a distinguishing feature, perhaps, of the principal artistic trends in our century that each of them has, in fact, offered a vocabulary, one that has lent a certain uniformity of style to artists however contrasted in character. I have suggested earlier that this kind of uniformity—'type-forms', the 'existence of standards', to recall Gropius's convenient and pithy statements—is to be welcomed rather than deplored; but so far as the Method was concerned, its 'uniformity', wildly exaggerated and always 'imposed' upon the composers, was used as a stick with which to beat it. We meet something of the same sort in a not unfamiliar approach to Cubism which, like the Method, has been reproached for impersonal mechanics which supposedly leave 'little room for the play of the artist's individual sensibility'. But as Sir Herbert Read, on continuing, remarks, 'Actually, nothing could be more distinct than the personality, the individuality, of the work of the various cubist painters I have mentioned [among them, Gris, Picasso, Braque, Matisse, Léger, Delaunay]. No one would ever confuse a work by Braque with a work by Léger'.[1] Nor, of course, would it be possible not to distinguish one serial composer from another. If one thinks for a moment only of Schoenberg, Berg and Webern, and their serial compositions, how crystal clear is the exposure of an 'individual sensibility' in each case; and yet there is no denying that the common use of a serial language does constitute a genuine community of language. Of course, today we tend, rightly, to stress the artistic independence of each member of the famous trinity, especially in the case of Webern, whose own narrow path has been so widely opened up and further developed by the succeeding generation of Webernites. None the less, how true it remains that, given a comprehensive understanding of Schoenberg, most of Berg and by no means the inessentials of Webern are clear to us. The 'uniformity' of the Method, however radically different the application, does help one to bridge, though it does not conceal, wide contrasts in artistic character and intent. This same uniformity and contrast is certainly evident in the Cubist painters, and even well outside their group; something of the potential consistency of the language is demonstrated in the work of those painters who, in fact, were only momentarily under its spell, or at least the spell of it as a complete vocabulary. An example, perhaps, is Chagall, a painter of the strongest personal flavour in inspiration and

---

[1] Read, *op. cit.*, pp. 97–8.

style; and yet his paintings from the years when he was obviously influenced by the Cubist movement—things like *The Soldier drinks* (1912–13), *Calvary* (1912) or the explicit *Paysage cubiste* (1918)[1]—while they speak the instantaneously recognizable Cubist language, are in no way uncharacteristic of his art: they are no less immediately recognizable as Chagall. (It is typical of him, indeed, that his 'abstract' Cubist landscape is peopled, literally so, with human furniture: a little man, in a street scene, is planted solidly among the void, intersecting planes.) That Chagall would move on from Cubism was predictable, maybe. What should interest us here was the need he felt at this time for 'new means' with which to give shape to his as yet 'formless' future creations, and the success with which the principles of Cubism functioned as the new means for which he was searching. He was hungry for a vocabulary, and it was a vocabulary that Cubism provided.[2]

The very fact that painters so various could avail themselves of a technique which lent their work, however distinct, an undeniable uniformity, is suggestive of the method that could be deduced from the empirical practice of Cubism's founders. Both Picasso and Braque *painted* their innovations: they did not calculate them. One may agree that the reduction of what has been spontaneously created to a formula is always unwelcome; but the assembly of a vocabulary would seem to be an altogether different affair, not the dead letter of the law but the living parts of it. Despite the protestations of Picasso and Braque that Cubism was not a *system*, it is clearly evident that a *method* was, in fact, implicitly part of the language. (The distinction between system and method we owe to Schoenberg.) A primarily 'rational' painter like Juan Gris was, indeed, able to systematize the method and yet transcend it, as both Picasso and Braque acknowledge.[3]

---

[1] See Walter Erben: *Marc Chagall*, London, 1957, plates 9, 13, 20.
[2] Ibid., p. 36.   [3] Richardson, *op. cit.*, p. 9.

Perspective Renounced

I do not wish to press the parallel between Cubism and the serial method to idiotic lengths. What one may gain by an appraisal of movements in two arts can well be lost if, in the excitement of the pursuit of 'significant' correspondences, one begins to mistake one art for the other. Legitimate exaggeration in the cause of making a valid point must not blind one to the fact that music is music, and painting, painting. None the less, even when one bears this warning in mind, there seems to me to be a wealth of detail and a handful of more sizeable analogies which enable us, with reasonable confidence, to point to Cubism and Schoenberg's Method as comparable manifestations; their patterns of behaviour coincide at too many important points for the concurrence to be brushed aside.

Perhaps now the most important conclusion may be drawn.

Picasso's *Demoiselles* (1907) 'is . . . the logical point to begin a history of Cubism'. The painting is not yet Cubist, 'but many of the problems that faced Picasso and Braque in their creation of the style are stated here, clumsily perhaps, but clearly for the first time'. Most important, it is this canvas in which we encounter the 'dismissal of a system of perspective which had conditioned Western painting since the Renaissance', an innovation which marks 'the beginning of a new era in the history of art'.[1] The principle which had served as a rule was here displaced.

Thenceforth, perspective was progressively renounced.

Schoenberg's second string quartet, op. 10 (1907–8), is no less of a logical point from which to embark upon a survey of the steps which led him subsequently to the development of the serial method (steps which comprised its development, indeed). The work, as Erwin Stein remarks,

---

[1] John Golding: *Cubism, A History and an Analysis, 1907–14*, London, 1959, pp. 47, 58.

'marks a turning point in Schoenberg's compositions. He had looked across the borders of a tonality governed by a central key. . . .'[1] In the finale of the quartet we encounter him outward bound from tonality, upon the verge of the 'dismissal of a system which had conditioned Western music since the seventeenth century'. We might further adapt Dr. Golding's words to describe the quartet as 'the beginning of a new era in the history of music'. The principle which had served as a rule was here displaced.

Thenceforth, tonality was progressively renounced.

The abandonment of tonality and perspective. These gestures, surely, are not only comparable, but also equivalent? Have we not here a clear and pertinent example of patterns of development in two arts so alike in shape that the unity of feeling which governed the period of their mutual unfolding seems to be made tangible in terms of sound and paint?

If we trace the development of Cubism and serial music to the present day, the parallel appears to me to lose none of its significance. Cubism was not abstract in intent; at least, abstraction formed no part of the intention of its founders. On the other hand, there is no doubt that it was apparent at an early stage that Cubism opened up the possibility of abstraction. Apollinaire, Dr. Golding tells us, saw complete abstraction as the goal of Cubism,[2] and he points out later that many painters, during the first war, 'had come to see in Cubism only the first step towards a completely abstract form of painting'.[3] Now, of course, abstraction in the visual arts is encountered everywhere, an international style, it would seem, indubitably fathered by Cubism (itself, perhaps, as Dr. Golding remarks, *not* an international style, and misrepresented, in principle, by its abstract offspring).

---

[1] Stein, *op. cit.*, p. 51.   [2] *Op. cit.*, p. 34.   [3] *Op. cit.*, pp. 183–4.

Two Great Negative Gestures

Picasso, we know, passed through a hermetic period of Cubism (1910), perhaps again stimulated by Braque's example, but his work was never completely non-representational; he never wholly abandoned the object. Later, in the early years of the first world war, a critical period of transition for the Cubist movement, Picasso 'continued on the one hand to paint pictures with even greater severity and geometric precision and on the other to surprise and anger the more consistent but less talented artists by making drawings which were almost photographic in their naturalism'.[1]

It is impossible not to be strongly reminded of Schoenberg in this context. The Method, too, had its strict hermetic period—a profoundly impressive product of it was Schoenberg's wind quintet, op. 26 (1923–4)—and it is not hard to understand why both it and Cubism required a period of intensive discipline in the new techniques.

I have suggested earlier that the abandonment of tonality *abjures* rather than *asserts*. Likewise the abandonment of perspective. The proof here lies, surely, in the very fact of the development of Cubism and the Method? In each case, a new means, a new language, was unfolded, to provide the possibility of continued organization within the context of the new style. It is in this sense, I think, that we may regard both Picasso's and Schoenberg's individual acts of renunciation as the two great *negative* gestures which mark the history of the arts in the early years of the twentieth century. The *positive* reparations followed later, complementing what had been necessarily displaced.

As for Picasso's naturalistic essays, which commingle so pungently with canvases in a severe Cubist manner, is this seeming contradiction not very close to the pattern of behaviour we find in Schoenberg, who felt free similarly to juxtapose his modes of perception? Are we not reminded of

---

[1] Penrose, *op. cit.*, p. 189.

his compositions in the 'old style', of the explicit return to
tonality which he made in some works of the years of his
serial maturity? (I do not mean those late serial works in
which tonal elements play a constructive if strictly de-
limited rôle. This significant synthesis represents a new
style, a reconciliation perhaps, but not a return to a
'bygone aesthetic'.)

But Schoenberg, of course, could afford to relax, once
the Method was securely established. First, it had to be
shown, creatively, that the new principle *was* capable of
serving as a rule. Hence, the Method's hermetic period, to
which belong the piano suite, op. 25, and the wind quintet, op. 26—'. . . from the technical point of view . . . a real
compendium of the new possibilities; they are the classical
works of the twelve-note technique'.[1]

In the same way, the strict period of Cubism (1910) was
a necessary stage in the movement's development. The
language of a new style must establish itself fully in its
own right: it must of necessity be strict before it can be
free. A rule cannot first be demonstrated in terms of
exceptions to it. It was only from a position of linguistic
strength—with the achievement of a 'precisely definable
aesthetic control' (Schoenberg to Hauer)[2]—that Schoenberg and Picasso could later 'negotiate' with the past;
Schoenberg could readmit tonality, Picasso concern himself more overtly with the realism that Cubist painters
claimed as the basis of their art. The parallel between
hermetic periods,[3] their origins and consequences, seems
to me to hold true for both Cubism and the Method.

---

[1] H. H. Stuckenschmidt: *Arnold Schoenberg*, trans. E. T. Roberts and H. Searle,
London, 1959, pp. 88–9.

[2] *Briefe*, p. 109; but defined, of course, in works, not manifestos!

[3] I must emphasize here that the parallel resides primarily in the need of both
Cubism and the Method for a hermetic period in which, as it were, the rules of the
game were published. An important side-consequence of this in the case of Cubism
was the abstract vista it opened up, though this was not part of the intention of
the movement's founder-painters. As I shall suggest later, an abstract potentiality
is inherent in the serial method, but it was not a pronounced aspect of Schoenberg's

The Turn to Abstraction

But it can be objected to all this that the chronology of the two movements after the first stirrings of 1907 does not run parallel in any way whatsoever. It was not until 1921 that Schoenberg was able to formulate the Method which had painfully and slowly evolved since the war years. By then, Cubism had flowered, flourished and, as a strict, self-contained language, already become something of a 'classical' language (in T. S. Eliot's sense of 'classical'); its potentiality as a discipline was exhausted, its founders, Picasso and Braque, had themselves ventured upon new paths, though both artists, of course, have continued to register the impact of their heroic Cubist days.

To me this 'staggered' parallel suggests that the time-scales upon which music and visual arts operate are not identical. Painting, as it were, lives through its history, its innovations, its styles, even more swiftly than does music. There may be very good reasons why the eye is able to assimilate new modes of expression more quickly and easily than the ear. In any event, perspective could be renounced, a new visual language organized, and eventually relinquished, all within the space of a few years. Music, however, was slower to cut itself free from tonality, and slower still to build up a new means of order; which is suggestive of the relative slowness with which basic innovations in music evolve.

It is a mistake, however, to talk as if Cubism were a spent force. It may be that abstract art in a very real sense is a betrayal of the realist spirit which informed the work of Picasso and Braque. But no one can deny that abstract art could never have happened *without* Cubism; as I have already pointed out, the vista of abstraction was already opened up in Braque's and Picasso's hermetic period. What was a potent side-issue has now itself become a principle.

---

hermetic period. In short, I do not want to imply that 'hermetic' and 'abstract' are necessarily the same things, though one accompanied the other in the development of Cubism.

Abstract art has been with us for a very long time and shows signs of increasing rather than diminishing; and in the sense that Cubism is the 'parent of all abstract art forms',[1] Cubism is still with us today. (Mr. John Berger, in an article entitled 'The Myth of the Artist', pertinently observes, '. . . cubism supplies the possibility of a really modern contemporary living tradition of art, yet cubism is taught in no official London art school'.[2] The same observation, alas, may be made of the Method and our official schools of music.)

What provides, perhaps, the most interesting parallel between developments in music and painting is just this tendency towards abstraction. For can it be doubted that some of the newest of the new music—the post-Webern school of serial composition—is not intentionally and defiantly 'abstract' in a manner certainly not sanctioned by its father-founders and even perhaps in a manner which has previously not formed part of the composer's ambition in the whole history of music? That music has, so to speak, followed in the footsteps of painting at a not inconsiderable distance in time, would only seem to bear out my contention that different time-scales serve the two arts.

We know that abstract painting represents a deviation, however significant, from the principles of Cubism. In the same way, it seems to me, the post-Webernite New may well come to be regarded as a perversion rather than a natural outcome of the Method. Stuckenschmidt truly remarks that 'Schoenberg's melodic invention remained unchanged in its character from his first works to his last. It is the true substance of his music and of its invention.'[3] One might add that the possibility of melodic regeneration secured by the serial principle was a consequence of the utmost importance, since the progressive enfeeblement of

---

[1] P. and L. Murray: *A Dictionary of Art and Artists*, Penguin Books, 1959.

[2] *Artist, Critic and Teacher*, Joint Council for Education through Art, London, n.d., p. 21.   [3] *Op. cit.*, p. 25.

tonality had, inevitably and proportionally, enfeebled melody. The Method, then, was—or could be—a guarantee that melody, and, more importantly, the thematic process dependent upon thematic invention, need not die.

Schoenberg's music is 'about' its melody (I use the term here to include the whole thematic process). However 'absolute' his music may be, the question 'what is it about?' can always be put, and, in this 'absolute' sense, receive a meaningful answer: 'It is about these themes and their development.' This answer—the possibility of an answer—enables us to make a useful distinction: *absolute music is not the same as abstract music.* 'Absolute' and 'abstract' have often been loosely used in the context of music, as if their meaning were the same. I suggest that we should do well not to confuse the terms. 'Absolute' seems to me to serve well in its familiar rôle as label for music without programme, 'Music which is dissociated from extramusical implications' (*Harvard Dictionary of Music*). 'Abstract', I would suggest, belongs properly to that music of our own time which is athematic—'about' what?

One might think 'about nothing', and be right; and still earn the agreement of the composer. The witness of Karlheinz Stockhausen (b. 1928) is curiously negative. So many abjurations in so small a space!

Thus no recapitulation, no variation, no development. All that presupposes 'formal procedures'—themes and motives that are repeated, varied, developed, contrasted, worked out . . . All that I have abandoned since the first purely pointilliste works.[1]

It would be rash at this early stage to pronounce upon the claims or achievements of Stockhausen and composers like him. But two comments seem permissible. First, that it is the abolition of melody—or its attempted total abolition—that constitutes for the listener the overriding obstacle to comprehension of the works of the youngest

---

[1] Quoted in the *Observer*, October 11th, 1959, p. 24.

generation. It is true, of course, that modern music has often been chastised for its tunelessness, often wrongly so: it is now more readily recognized that Schoenberg, once the popular arch-enemy of tune, may more properly be regarded as its custodian. It is, in fact, only in the works of the most extreme post-Webernites that the old jibe—'it hasn't got a tune'—has become a reality. Modern music, at long last, succeeds in living up to its own bad reputation.

In taking this radical step it seems to me that music follows painting into abstraction in the sense that I have outlined above. To our equation of *tonality* and *perspective* we may now add another suggestive coupling: *theme* and *object*.

The picture, more than anything else, was 'about' its object(s); the composition, more than anything else, was 'about' its theme(s).[1] One is not so naive as to suppose that either work of art is not 'about' other things as well, of very great importance. But does one go so far wrong in suggesting that object and theme represent a comparable 'reality' about which the viewer or listener primarily builds his comprehension?

This brings me to my second and last point—that melody has, in fact, proved more tenacious than one would have thought possible. Whatever Pierre Boulez (b. 1925) may imagine he has accomplished in the way of athematic music, it is curious how obstinately melody remains a feature of his works. Certainly he achieves a high degree of freedom from thematic procedures in the instrumental accompaniment of a work like the second *Improvisation sur Mallarmé* ('Une dentelle s'abolit': the choice of poem and poet is significant), but the

---

[1] About its harmony too, of course, and its rhythm. But is not melody often the composer's method of making audible in a particularly lucid way the stages of development in his tonal structure? Is this not why monothematicism in the sonata gave way to dual-thematicism? Why the dominant stage in the tonal argument came to be marked, in fact, by a 'contrasting' second subject? Is this not a clear instance of harmony, as it were, explaining itself—making its function clear—in terms of melody?

soprano part relies upon melodic arabesques that are surprisingly conventional in conception. A failure of imagination here, one might think, of which a consequence is a distinct conflict between voice and instrumental context; the latter is improvisational in effect, the former not improvisational enough. In any event, the thread around which the fragmented texture coheres is a melodic one; and in Boulez's *Le marteau sans maître* one finds much the same kind of thing—the voice or flute sustains a flow of melodic imagery which knits together the textures of the vocal or instrumental numbers.[1]

Possibly Boulez is, in a sense, too good a composer, too much of a natural composer, to make a complete success of the doctrine of his own school.[2] It is not, however, altogether surprising that it is a French composer who has become so prominent among the latter-day abstractionists. There is no doubt that the late works of Debussy already hint at a possibly athematic music. One finds this trend latent in piano works, e.g., the *Etudes*, and the ballet, *Jeux*. It was not only from Webern that Boulez learned of music's abstract potentialities. Debussy has been mentioned before as one of the father-figures in the history of the modern movement in music. The condition to which he brought his music at the end of his life clearly foreshadows the work of what one might call the second Parisian school. There is a parallel here with Cézanne; both composer and painter, unknowingly but decisively, offered a

---

[1] Long after writing this paragraph I find my supposition confirmed by Mr. Robert Craft in the notes that accompany his recorded performance of *Le marteau* (Philips 'Modern Music' Series): 'the music is all melody, basically', he writes.

[2] i.e., '... rhythmic and melodic *dis*continuity, "*irrational*" rhythm, "athematicism", *non*-tonality, as well as the notion of constantly evolving forms': André Hodeir, in *Since Debussy, A View of Contemporary Music*, London, 1961, p. 123. Amusingly enough, though perhaps expectedly so, M. Hodeir finds that Boulez's *Le marteau* falls short of these negative ideals. It is not without significance that the only work by an *avant-garde* composer to achieve any kind of popularity should give rise to patent turbulence in the breasts of Boulez's most ardent disciples.

glimpse of a future which has become very much our present. The singularity of this fact is intensified by these great artists' popular reputation as Impressionists, an aesthetic which they themselves outlived in their own works and which now plays a negligible rôle in music and painting.

III

STRAVINSKY: THE PAST
MADE ACCESSIBLE TO
NEW FEELING

But where does Stravinsky fit into a picture—my picture
—that has hitherto been dominated by the Method? It is
only in the music of his latest (last?) phase, from 1953
to the present time, that he has adopted serial procedures,
an astonishing turn of the historical wheel that finally
unites, under a common roof, the music of the two
great masters of the twentieth century. No neater
dénouement could have been devised by the most tidy-
minded of historians.

Up to the 1950s, however, up to the composition, above
all, of the symphonies (1940 and 1945), and *The Rake's
Progress* (1948/51), Stravinsky might well have greeted
the proponents of the Method with the words (probably
not the tune) of a once popular song: 'I get along without
you very well.' For so he had, in a whole series of master
works which we recognize as the rich harvest of his neo-
classical period, a descriptive term that the composer
himself does not disallow.

It was not Stravinsky, after all, who 'invented' neo-
classicism, though one may concede the point that he has
proved its most persistent—and successful—advocate. The
seeds of the movement are already beginning to stir in the
late romantic composers, in Brahms, in Wagner's *Meister-*

singer, in Strauss's *Ariadne* (strong in neo-classical theory, at any rate, if not in practice), and most overtly in the uncomfortably hybrid works of Busoni.[1] 'Models', if one may so put it, were in the air. A shove, or stimulus from the past, might well, if one was a composer, pitch one into the future, or at least provide one with a foothold amid the ever-changing, dissolving sands of styles, quicksands indeed, that threatened to engulf rather than support a creative talent in the early decades of this century.

How to go on? This was a question, a predicament, that was faced not only by all the composers of minor gifts but also by the major figures, Bartók, Hindemith, Schoenberg (not less so, his pupils) and Stravinsky. *Le roi est mort! Vive le roi!* But if the royal line, the tradition, is extinguished, how does one set about hailing a successor?

Reaction, anti-tradition, as I have already suggested, will carry one so far, but not far enough; gestures in this field, however major in achievement, however fruitful for the future of the art, of the creators concerned, always seem to contain a built-in limitation, a certain negative element. The emancipated rhythms of *Le Sacre* and the non-tonal 'freedom' of *Erwartung*, for instance, provided neither Stravinsky nor Schoenberg with a vocabulary sufficiently rich in resources to meet, in full, the demands of their future development as artists. Despite the wealth of new and fertile ground explored in each case, both composers had, in a sense, to begin afresh; Schoenberg to grow into the Method, Stravinsky to evolve a relation with the past. Thus side by side the two main streams of the New in music developed.

But can we, in fact, treat the Method and neo-classicism as if they were comparable phenomena? It would seem to me that here a clear distinction must be made if confusion is to be avoided. In a sense, I think one can

---

[1] Some movements of Mahler (the finale of the seventh symphony, for example, the Minuet of the third, and the Rondo Burleske of the ninth) show neo-classical leanings; and one cannot overlook the kinship of Reger and Hindemith.

speak of the one as a language, the other as a style. The Method, if one may so describe it, is a strictly neutral instrument of creation. It offers the possibility of a language, of a common vocabulary, but imposes no conditions of personality (aside from the composer's own). Neoclassicism, on the other hand, by its very nature, introduces an element of personality (the chosen model or style from the past) that is not the composer's own, though one need scarcely stress how profoundly, in Stravinsky's case, he makes the 'alien' component his own. One may justly claim, however, that the kind of singular gratification that one gains from a neo-classical work depends upon an act of double-recognition, of both a model (even if we cannot name it) and the composer's transformation of it. (Is this not true, for instance, of Stravinsky's Gluck-like, seraphic *Persephone?*)

Stravinsky himself has argued that neo-classicism embraced not only his own music but most of his great contemporaries': 'Every age', he observes, 'is a historical unity. It may never appear as anything but either/or to its partisan contemporaries, of course, but semblance is gradual, and in time either and or come to be components of the same thing. For instance, "neo-classic" now begins to apply to all of the between-the-war composers (not that notion of the neo-classic composer as someone who rifles his predecessors and each other and then arranges the theft in a new "style"). The music of Schoenberg, Berg and Webern in the twenties was considered extremely iconoclastic at that time but these composers now appear to have used musical form as I did, "historically". My use of it was overt, however, and theirs elaborately disguised. (Take, for example, the *Rondo* of Webern's *Trio*; the music is wonderfully interesting but no one hears it as a Rondo.) We all explored and discovered new music in the twenties, of course, but we attached it to the very tradition we were so busily outgrowing a decade before.'[1]

---

[1] *Conversations*, p. 126. If the rondo character of Webern's Rondo is, in fact,

Stravinsky's Discovery of the Past

There are, surely, some questionable aspects of this statement? Stravinsky rightly deprecates the naivety of the popular conception of the neo-classical composer. But it can hardly be denied that neo-classical procedures, however subtle, entail a deliberate preoccupation with the past. Stravinsky himself, in words that show a care for the complexities of the issues involved, expresses the 'notion' thus, in *Memories and Commentaries* (page 110):

> My instinct is to recompose, and not only students' works, but old masters' as well. When composers show me their music for criticism all I can say is that I would have written it quite differently. Whatever interests me, whatever I love, I wish to make my own (I am probably describing a rare form of kleptomania).

This brilliant flash of self-examination (but what is the distinction between thieving (or rifling) and kleptomania?) is part of an answer to a question from Mr. Craft about teaching. The general sense of it, however, informs Stravinsky's later observations on *Le Baiser de la fée* and *Pulcinella*, in *Expositions and Developments*:[1]

> I believe, with Auden, that the only critical exercise of value must take place in, and by means of, art, i.e., in pastiche or parody; *Le Baiser de la fée* and *Pulcinella* are music criticisms of this sort, though more than that, too.

> *Pulcinella* was my discovery of the past, the epiphany through which the whole of my late work became possible. It was a backward look, of course—the first of many love affairs in that direction—but it was a look in the mirror, too. No critic understood this at the time, and I was therefore attacked for being a *pasticheur*, chided for composing 'simple' music, blamed for deserting 'modernism', accused of renouncing my 'true Russian heritage'. People who had never heard of, or cared about, the originals cried 'sacrilege': 'The classics are ours. Leave the classics alone.' To them all, my answer was and is the same: You 'respect', but I love.

---

inaudible, one wonders if it may be legitimately described as even a disguised example of neo-classicism. In *Memories and Commentaries*, p. 122, Stravinsky refers to three 'neo-classic' schools, ascendant from 1930 to 1945—Schoenberg's, Hindemith's and his own.

[1] Pp. 109, 113–14.

There could be no clearer statements, one might think, of Stravinsky's unequivocally positive attitude to the past, which obliges him to compose to a 'model' or 'personality' as part of his natural composing process. We are, in truth, continually faced in Stravinsky's neo-classical works by the 'recomposing' of which he himself has spoken; and his 'love', we may note, need not exclude an element of objective criticism. Indeed, both affection and aggression are involved in his 'love affairs'.[1]

Of one thing we may be absolutely certain; that there has not been a case like Stravinsky's in any previous period of musical history. Up to a point, of course, the past has always had a rôle to play in every composer's music. The emerging master (Beethoven, say) has composed against the background of his predecessors (Haydn and Mozart in Beethoven's case, the former particularly), even aggressively so (Beethoven again). One might claim that affection had rather less to do with the relationship of a classical composer to his 'models'. He wished, in a sense, to develop *away* from them, to triumph *over* them. Even the passive Mozart: are we to imagine that he did not enjoy writing all those indifferent eighteenth-century composers out of existence, whose clichés appear, immeasurably transformed, in his own music? That Bach, for that matter, did not savour his 'recompositions' of Vivaldi?

It is plain, indeed, that Stravinsky felt something of this kind of pleasure himself when writing *Pulcinella* and *Le Baiser* ('music criticisms . . . though more than that, too'). But what radically divorces Stravinsky from any classical precedents one may have in mind is the immense distance in time that separates him from 'his' past. It was their immediate predecessors who were the concern of composers in earlier times. But not so for Stravinsky, for whom the immediate past, both in general and in particular (his 'true Russian heritage'), was soon to be

---

[1] A point made in Hans Keller's 'Towards the Psychology of Stravinsky's Genius', *The Listener*, November 29th, 1956.

abandoned as a major influence in his music. (The *Firebird*, which the world will rightly continue to value more highly than its composer, might be considered, in some respects, as a 'criticism' of Rimsky-Korsakov. It is in this early work, in fact, that one encounters, almost for the last time, that immediate continuity—expansion—criticism of a tradition that had hitherto been characteristic of musical history. One does not really meet it again in Stravinsky until the present day, when his serial works bring him in relation to a 'past' that is closer to him in time than have any of the 'backward looks' of his strictly neo-classical period.)

One may well wonder, on a superficial reading of the facts, how this past-obsessed period in Stravinsky's long creative life may be classified as a manifestation of the New. But one can only—and mistakenly—think of Stravinsky as curator of a private museum if one closes one's ears to the sound of his neo-classical music, which affirms in every bar his own statement that 'a new piece of music *is* a new reality'.[1] It has now become a cliché to remark upon Stravinsky's ability to remain himself whatever 'model' he cares to adopt, but the cliché is none the less true because it happens to form part of the vocabulary of almost every commentator on Stravinsky's music. The validity of the cliché even survives the difficulty that many commentators find in pinning the right model to the right work. One encounters a typical confusion in the responses to Stravinsky's violin concerto (1931), a shamefully neglected work,[2] in the two slow Arias of which the composer, for me at least, offers some of his deepest and most finely poised 'classical' inspirations; so finely poised, indeed, that no one can decide which models are involved. ('Tansman and Strobel', writes Roman Vlad, 'have mentioned the name of Bach, Casella that of Weber, while others have even spoken of Tchai-

---

[1] *Expositions*, p. 102.   [2] Less so now (1965).

kovsky.'[1] Mr. Vlad does not commit himself to an opinion;
I should plump for Bach.) Much the same kind of muddle
confronts us if we seek for a consensus of opinion about the
'sources' of *The Rake's Progress*. It is not unusual to come
across rival claims made on behalf of the model that has
supposedly served Stravinsky as a springboard in a particular aria.

The very problem of precise recognition emphasizes the
wealth and scope of Stravinsky's references and reminds us
of the powers of transformation his wonderful genius
enjoys. None the less, the *fact* (or presence) of the models
remains, whether we recognize them or not, whether they
are explicit (as in *Pulcinella* or *Le Baiser*) or concealed (as
in the violin concerto or a dozen other works); we sense
them—feel them—even if we cannot pin them down (we
can't wish them away). We feel them, I suggest, and
rightly so, not as quotations or face-lifts or the donning of
masks (all aspects of neo-classical practice very different
from Stravinsky's own, and some of them certainly dis-
reputable), but as the natural and perfect expression of
Stravinsky's feelings *about* the past; which brings me to
what I take to be the crux of the matter.

For what Stravinsky has achieved in his neo-classical
music seems to me to fall very much into line with what we
have already observed as characteristic of manifestations
of the New elsewhere, in both music and the other arts: the
exploration of new worlds of feeling, or, to put it more
accurately, and once more to return to Giedion's unique
insight, making 'new parts of the world . . . accessible to
feeling'.[2] *The 'new' part of the (musical) world that Stravinsky has made accessible to active creative feeling is no less*

---

[1] *Stravinsky*, trans. Frederick and Ann Fuller, London, 1960, p. 115.

[2] Giedion, *op. cit.*, p. 427. We find a perfect example in literature of what Giedion
has in mind; Dickens's incorporation of the Railway Age into his novels, a new
world which he made 'accessible to feeling' in, and through, a whole battery of
new poetic images. This specific achievement is fully documented in *The Dickens
World*, Humphry House, second edition, London, 1942, pp. 137–45.

than the past itself. This extraordinary act may have had its historical precedents, as I have already suggested, and even been shared among Stravinsky's great contemporaries to a degree that enables one to write sensibly of a 'movement' (the 'unity of feeling' to which I have referred before). But the more deeply one dives into Stravinsky's neo-classical music, the clearer it becomes that his achievement is not only greater, more serious and more significant than that of any other composer working in this field, but also wholly distinct in kind. The 'movement', in fact, would seem to belong to its minor practitioners, not to its master, Stravinsky.

This would seem to contradict what the composer himself has written in the passage quoted above, where Stravinsky shrewdly—but perhaps a little self-defensively—points out that the serial composers, too, showed neo-classical tendencies. One cannot doubt that this is, up to a point, a perfectly just comment; think, for instance, of Berg's wellnigh manic obsession with traditional formal procedures in *Wozzeck* or of Schoenberg's lifelong pre-occupation with classical sonata form. But though one may wish to agree with Stravinsky that one meets here a hidden but none the less 'historical' use of form (much more so in Berg than in Schoenberg, who, by the way, was not above a mild bout of archaizing now and again in the manner that is most generally associated with neo-classicism, e.g., in his *Serenade*, op. 24),[1] it is hard to place the neo-classicism of Schoenberg and his 'school' and the neo-classicism of Stravinsky on an equal footing. That there was a certain 'unity of feeling' none may deny, but it was surely not more than a semblance? After all, if we play Stravinsky alongside Schoenberg, or Berg, it is not a

---

[1] In some respects the most overtly neo-classical work Schoenberg wrote was his Suite for string orchestra in G major (1934), one of his later tonal compositions. It is not without significance, I think, that the return to tonality posed a problem of *style* that was solved, in part at least, by the adoption of some characteristic neo-classical features.

common attitude to the past that strikes us as a unifying principle in their music.

For a start, one finds that it is not 'neo-classicism' (in the sense of the term that one applies to Stravinsky's music) that flies to one's lips (or pen) when describing the senior serial composers. Is it not 'tradition' that one falls back on—that one experiences, indeed, in their music? (I notice that I have used 'traditional' already, when writing about Berg.) A sense of tradition was certainly strong in these men, particularly in Schoenberg, as we were recently reminded by Roberto Gerhard:

Schoenberg's sense of belonging to a tradition and of working in the main stream of that tradition is alive in every phase of his evolution, even at his most boldly innovating.[1]

Despite the radical innovations in language, in fact, the sense of tradition persists and expresses itself most powerfully in the maintenance of traditional forms, however much expanded or reformulated. Tradition, indeed, was a 'live' issue for Schoenberg and his pupils as it never was, never has been, for Stravinsky. One exaggerates only a little I think if, holding in mind the characteristic forms of Schoenberg and Berg, one discerns a relation between them and their past not very different in kind from that which we have noted as a general feature of composers throughout the history of music. They composed, in short, against the background of the past (the immediate past, even if we are prepared to accept that 'immediate', for the Viennese composer, means Beethoven and Brahms, not to speak of Haydn and Mozart), in the tradition of their eminent forebears. One meets here not so much neo-classicism as a continuation of the classical heritage.

Stravinsky himself would seem to be aware that he stands in a very different relation to tradition. He was, and has remained, tradition-less:

I was guided by no system whatever in *Le Sacre du printemps*. When

---

[1] Article in the *Sunday Telegraph*, December 3rd, 1961, p. 11.

Stravinsky and Symphony

I think of the other composers of that time who interest me—Berg, who is synthetic (in the best sense), Webern, who is analytic, and Schoenberg, who is both—how much more *theoretical* their music seems than *Le Sacre*; and these composers were supported by a great tradition, whereas very little immediate tradition lies behind *Le Sacre du printemps*. I had only my ear to help me. I heard and I wrote what I heard. I am the vessel through which *Le Sacre* passed.[1]

Stravinsky, we may note, with interest, uses the term 'great tradition' of his contemporaries, the very feature that, I suggest, distinguishes their kind of (traditional) neo-classicism from his (non-traditional); and if, indeed, we look no further than the 'historical' use of form—which Stravinsky seems to regard as a link between his 'school' and Schoenberg's—we find very little there to support a theory of common practice, overt on the one hand and hidden on the other. For Stravinsky's forms, on the whole, have steered clear of the classical Viennese tradition of 'symphony' which so obsessed Schoenberg and his pupils.[2]

---

[1] *Expositions*, pp. 147–8.

[2] The most important exceptions, I suppose, are the *Symphony in C* (1940) and the *Symphony in Three Movements* (1945), and magnificently substantial and successful exceptions they are, too. But one notes that Stravinsky waited a long time before making his approach to the sonata idea, and that it was not many years after the composition of these works that his neo-classical period reached its terminus (*The Rake's Progress*, 1948/51); thereafter, his music moved into the period of transition that finally culminated in his adoption of the Method. In a sense, one might view the unexpectedly close thematic development of the symphonies as a natural step on the path towards serial procedures. But Stravinsky tackled the problem of 'classical' form in his own inimitable fashion. Though he chose to challenge the later Viennese composers on their home ground—'symphony' —his triumph was achieved strictly in his own triumphantly diatonic terms; he not only showed a profound consciousness of the tradition that had been the special preserve of the Schoenberg 'school' but made it explicit in the very language that his great Viennese contemporaries had abandoned: tonality. These extraordinary works, which are among Stravinsky's greatest, demonstrate in a most striking manner the composer's capacity to make the past accessible to the present in a new way. Who would have thought it possible that 'symphony' might be thus re-felt in the mid-twentieth century? At the same time, Stravinsky is nowhere more recognizably 'himself' than in these works, above all in the *Symphony in Three Movements*. Both symphonies are so central to any consideration of Stravinsky's art, and so revealing of its essence, that more must be said about them on a later page (see p. 114). But this observation, perhaps, belongs here: that 'symphony', in a sense, was the culminating point, the *Höhepunkt*, of his neo-

Abstention from Classical Forms

(If they owe anything to tradition at all, it is to the music of Debussy that we must turn for an example of a senior composer anticipating Stravinsky's innovations, though at a late stage in Debussy's career it seems as if he were influenced, in turn, by Stravinsky.)[1] The anti-developmental characteristics of his instrumental music have often been commented on (e.g., the sectional development through block contrasts of the *Symphonies of Wind Instruments*). No less telling a pointer in its way is the high proportion of works in Stravinsky's catalogue that have their roots in the musical theatre; in ballet, for example, in opera-oratorio (*Oedipus Rex*) or melodrama (*Persephone*), or in hybrid conceptions like *Les Noces* or *L'Histoire du soldat*; or there is the long—and still growing (*The Flood!*)[2]—list of sacred works that have their origins in biblical or religious texts (an interest Stravinsky has maintained in the decades that have passed since the composition of the *Symphony of Psalms*, and nowhere more strongly than in his serial phase). To whatever period of Stravinsky's music one turns, in fact, one finds the same abstention from the kind of classical forms that served Schoenberg and his 'school'. When one counts the differences on the one hand, and the similarities on the other, it is hard to conclude that a comparison of Schoenberg's and Stravinsky's 'historical' use of form shows many common features. There is a wide gulf, indeed, between Stravinsky's special sense of the 'past' and Schoenberg's no less special sense of 'immediate tradition'. Only an occasional meeting point remains.

If one surveys neo-classicism as it manifested itself in other composers (and none can deny the pervasiveness of

---

classicism. *This* world, already so elaborately documented by other composers and burdened with so formidable a 'history', must have presented the severest challenge to Stravinsky's genius; small wonder that he was slow in turning to it. Once it was mastered—made newly accessible to feeling—there were few worlds left to conquer; only the more recent 'past' of the Method.

[1] In *La Boîte à joujoux* (1913), for example.

[2] Even more recently, *Abraham and Isaac* (1963) and *Introitus* (1965).

the phenomenon), Stravinsky's species seems all the more singular. For it was not for him, as for so many other composers, even for composers of genius—Bartók, Falla or Prokofiev, for example—a kind of stylistic face-lift; nor was it the kind of classical 'revival' that seems at first to have an element of the New about it and then exposes itself as the expression of an innate and even rather aggressive conservatism, a dreadful fate that has overtaken Hindemith, whose best music belongs to his earlier days as a composer, when he was least concerned with asserting 'tradition' as a holy mission and was not overwhelmed, as he appears to be today, by his own 'past'.

As Picasso has wittily observed, 'To copy others is necessary but to copy oneself is pathetic.' The very fact that Hindemith can be described in the following terms is disquieting: 'This bold, round, jovial little man . . . has mellowed during his 63 years into something of an elder statesman. In Germany in the 20s he was the scourge of bourgeois convention. No experiment was too daring for him. . . . Now he is a respectable university professor in America and a dispenser of robust wisdom to the young' (Adam Bell in the *Evening Standard*, November 21st, 1958). The terms are journalistic, of course, but, alas, they convey in capsule form the history of Hindemith's music.

Stravinsky's neo-classicism was none of these things, though it has been misunderstood and mispractised as all of them; hence, while it is true that he is the most influential figure in the neo-classical 'movement', he is also the most solitary, without imitators in any fundamental sense. His neo-classicism was, and remains, both radical and new, new, because his music was 'about' the past, not an attempt to revive it or extend it or transform it; nor to touch up a pre-existent style with classical 'features'. The past, in fact, for Stravinsky, enjoys the status of an 'object';[1] it is the 'theme' of his music in the

---

[1] One of the few realistic parallels between Stravinsky and Picasso may be discerned in their common approach to the past as 'object'. Picasso has always been

same sense that the musical theme, serially invigorated, was the 'object' of Schoenberg's music (see pages 90–2). Stravinsky's opening up of the past to new feelings presupposes a relation to the past (as object) of the order of Dickens's assimilation of the Railway Age (see page 101, note 2) or Gaudi's incorporation of the imagery of natural rock-formations into his architecture.

It may be objected, and quite properly, that to use the word 'theme' as I have used it in the last paragraph is to confuse two quite independent meanings. I concede the confusion and would seek to clarify it, without losing a meaningful identity of terminology, by stressing how 'theme-conscious', musically speaking, is Stravinsky's relation to the past. It is melody, indeed, which is the key to the secret of his neo-classical practice. The theme *of* the past is expressed, as it were, by means of the theme *from* the past.

It was some years ago now that Mr. Hans Keller, with remarkable perspicacity, defined the crisis in melody that was the result of the gradual enfeeblement of the tonal cadence.[1] Schoenberg, as we have seen, solved the crisis by the development of the Method. The abandonment of tonality having left him with no melodic resources but those of the most short-winded type, he was urged on to find a new means of reasserting the possibility of extended melody.

Stravinsky did not abandon tonality; on the contrary, he kept it alive during the long period (of more than two decades) when Schoenberg abstained from tonal references.[2] But he too was faced by a melodic crisis no less

---

open to classical stimuli, but perhaps his most 'Stravinskian' relation to the past may be found in his recent suite of paintings after Velasquez' *Las Meninas*.

[1] 'The Melodic Crisis', a sub-section of 'The Musical Character', in *Benjamin Britten*, a symposium edited by Donald Mitchell and Hans Keller, London, 1952, pp. 339–41.

[2] I have already referred (p. 70) to the complementary relations of Stravinsky and Schoenberg. If I prefer to regard them thus, rather than as antitheses (a more widespread habit), it is because their music so often presents a curiously com-

pressing than Schoenberg's. This was not only due to the natural development of his own music, above all by his concentration on rhythm as a leading principle of organization, but to his voluntary secession from the only 'immediate tradition' he knew, the tradition out of which he grew: his 'true Russian heritage', the school of Russian Nationalists. His abdication of his 'Russian' rôle meant that the resources of folksong, of national 'type-forms' (Gropius)—of which he had availed himself in his earlier music—were no longer at his disposal.[1]

This is the place, perhaps, for a necessary digression, since the mention of Stravinsky's 'Russian heritage' raises the whole issue of national music. A 'national' style, indeed, was yet another means of continuation available to composers after the turn of the century. What had been, in the nineteenth century, a kind of musical patriotism, superimposed on largely supra-national forms, developed in the twentieth into a large-scale movement. It was based on an approach to, or revival of, national materials more radical than anything the earlier nationalists had dreamed of, and its methods were defined in the works of an industrious body of composers, pre-eminent among them, of course, Bartók. The possibilities opened up by the rediscovery of folksong, in fact, must stand alongside neoclassicism and serial technique as the third and last of the

plementary division of interests. At one stage, for instance, it seemed as if we should always be required to recognize Schoenberg by his regenerated melodies and Stravinsky by his innovating rhythms.

[1] Stravinsky's 'Russian' period, however, lasted well beyond what most people take to be its climax—*Le Sacre*. (The real point of culmination was, surely, *Les Noces?*) *Renard* (1916/17) is virtually a pendant to *Le Sacre*, a miniature 'Rite' in both its music and its drama. (I have no doubt that the 'sacrificial' features of the story gave rise to the appropriately 'Rite'-like musical images.) Though the composer's Russian characteristics become progressively less explicit in the 'twenties and 'thirties, they continue to make unexpected appearances. For instance, there is the surprising and delightful chorus in *Persephone*, 'Nous apportons nos offrandes' (Fig. 207) which is as Russian in melodic character as it is characteristically Stravinskian in rhythmic structure. (One might similarly describe the 'Te Deum' in *The Flood*.)

'answers' to the question: 'How to go on?' (There is scarcely a composer in the first half of this century who has not allied himself to one of these 'schools', sometimes to more than one.)[1]

We may note at once that the 'folksong revival' was yet another means of circumventing the melodic crisis; derivations from, or actual specimens of, folksong provided the hard-pressed composer with a ready-made fund of fresh melody; and scarcely less important, tonality itself might be refreshed and fertilized by its contact with unusual modes, and rhythm revitalized by the asymmetry characteristic of the best folk-art. Does one not encounter here again the possibilities of a 'language' for music?

Many composers have undoubtedly thought so. If one turns at once to the example of Bartók, it is because he was, without question, the major figure working in this field, whose achievements, equally without question, were of a major order. Bartók was a man of genius, and if not quite of the stature of Schoenberg or Stravinsky, certainly a great modern master whose finest work, I have no doubt, will endure. Indeed, Bartók stands in relation to the folksong revival in much the same way as Stravinsky stands in relation to neo-classicism: he was the persistent advocate and most influential member of a widespread 'movement' which rarely matched—and as frequently misunderstood—his practice. We find, in fact, that Bartók's feelings 'about' folksong were as profound—and as consequential in their results—as Stravinsky's 'about' the past. Folksong was made accessible to feeling in quite a new way.[2]

---

[1] One's passion for pigeon-holing, however, must not lead one to overlook the odd-man-out composer, like Prokofiev, who, though substantially influenced by two of the principal 'schools', had the 'biological personality' (Stravinsky's term) to go it alone; but most of the misfits, if one may so describe them, despite their eclectic talent, were marginal figures.

[2] It is this aspect of Bartók's work, I feel, that distinguishes it from the achievement of minor practitioners like Kodály or our own Vaughan Williams, whose

Stravinsky himself appears to underrate Bartók's unique contribution to twentieth-century music in the

---

music laid a 'folksong revival' at our very door. But whereas with Bartók one is conscious of the New, especially in matters of rhythm and harmony (scarcely less innovating in their way than Stravinsky's), with, say, Vaughan Williams, the archaic element is much stronger; one often senses that he was *asserting* the past rather than demonstrating a new way of feeling about it. Both Bartók and Vaughan Williams, of course, were concerned with establishing a tradition free of an immediate (and alien) past. (What Bartók had to fight against was the skin-deep type of 'nationalism', a folkish mask imposed on an eclectic face. A perfect example of this uncomfortable stylistic situation is his own Second Suite for orchestra, op. 4.) But Bartók was aided in his affirmation of a unique, untainted past (the resources of Hungarian and related folksong) by the development of a new European 'present', which enabled him to avoid any hint of an attempt to re-assert 'lost' pastoral values. Vaughan Williams was not so fortunate, even if one leaves on one side all question of comparative talent. In England there was not, as there was in Europe, an emerging tradition concerned with the New. He did not even find himself heir to a tradition in a ripe state of disintegration in which intimations of the New are inherent; on the contrary, the musical scene in England after the turn of the century possessed all the immobility of a waxworks stacked with dummy composers and the effigies that they passed off as compositions. 'How to go on?' was not so much the question; it was, rather, 'How to go *back*?' For English music, such was its curious historical predicament, had to relive its past if it were ever to secure a future. It had, as it were, to start all over again. No one, I think, would wish to deny or diminish the importance of Vaughan Williams's act of rehabilitation, which restored an identity to English music and gave English composers' morale a much-needed boost. But it is difficult to escape the conclusion that he became in some sense a victim of his own achievement: encircled by the past, not freed by it. His attempts to widen his scope—e.g., the fourth symphony—suggest that he was intermittently conscious of the prison bars. Vaughan Williams's 'historical' use of folksong—how close it stands to the historical practice of the minor neo-classicists!—was undoubtedly influential. One wishes it had not in-fluenced a composer of the same generation, Gustav Holst, who had, in many ways, a more interesting musical mind than Vaughan Williams. Holst was perhaps the only English musician of his time to respond creatively to the early music of Stravinsky and, later, to the challenge of neo-classicism. But he was a strangely divided personality, and even his best music—works like *Egdon Heath* and the *Hammersmith* Prelude and Scherzo—are fatally flawed by the seemingly compul-sive introduction of folksong into essentially non-folklike (and often adventurous) contexts. Of Holst it may be truly said that he was born too soon. His highly interesting and imaginative language, at its best, was free of the insularity that plagued the folksong school. But, of course, it was just Holst's cosmopolitanism that was unwelcome in his own day. It is not surprising that even he himself seemed to have a bad conscience about it; hence, perhaps, the safeguarding, but disfiguring, capers into folksong in those works that are farthest from the village green.

most grotesque fashion. 'I knew the most important musician he was', he writes, 'I had heard wonders about the sensitivity of his ear, and I bowed deeply to his religiosity. However, I never could share his lifelong gusto for his native folklore. This devotion was certainly real and touching, but I couldn't help regretting it in the great musician.'[1]

'Lifelong gusto for his native folklore', a devotion 'real and touching'; these are phrases that might well apply to Vaughan Williams or Kodály but are scarcely adequate where Bartók is concerned.[2] One might as well regret in Stravinsky his gusto for the 'past', a devotion no less real or touching; and so indeed one might, if one listened to Stravinsky as Stravinsky apparently listens to Bartók; in both cases, it is principally by their melody that we recognize their allegiances, the 'past' on the one hand, folksong on the other; in both cases the crisis in melody was the agent that precipitated the choice of models.

That Stravinsky made one choice and Bartók another is doubtless due not so much to the shifts of history as to matters of individual genius, of the make-up of each composer's artistic personality.[3] How might Stravinsky have

---

[1] *Conversations*, p. 74. Stravinsky's own sensitive and omnivorous ear, none the less, has shown itself open to influence by Bartók in at least one prominent instance. Compare Fig. 153 (and later 191) in the finale of the *Symphony in Three Movements* (1945) with Fig. 200 in the scherzo of Bartók's *Music for Strings, Percussion and Celesta* (1936). The coincidence of rhythm, texture and instrumentation (piano!) is striking. There are certain finales of Bartók's, sometimes even those of his best works, where I feel that folk-derived music came too easily to him as a means of rounding off a piece; he allowed folklore, as it were, to do his composing for him. But it is surprising to find Stravinsky overlooking invention as personal in character as the crepuscular 'Night Music' that one so often encounters in Bartók's works (e.g., in the 'Elegia' of the Concerto for Orchestra). This was an empire of nocturnal sound which Bartók made peculiarly his own. One should also remember his pioneering achievements in the field of percussion.

[2] Schoenberg was not much more penetrating than Stravinsky in this matter. Though he does not mention Bartók by name in his deprecatory essay 'Folkloristic Symphonies' (1947), published in *Style and Idea*, it is hard to believe that he would not have had Bartók in mind when he wrote it.

[3] I found myself thinking of Stravinsky's neo-classical music when reading a

developed if he had chosen instead to devote himself wholly to his Russian heritage? Speculation, of course, is purposeless. But we may note that in his earlier music Stravinsky's relation to an immediate 'national' tradition was not so very different from Bartók's. Both, in any event, had to come to terms with it, Bartók by seizing it and making it his own, Stravinsky (eventually) by renouncing it.

This is not the place for a comparative study of Bartók and Stravinsky (nor am I the man to attempt it; I do not feel close enough to Bartók's music); but we may note that both composers, as emphatically opposed as they are in melodic character, share an innovatory approach to rhythm and harmony, the principles of which, if not the practice, have much in common. It was, after all, in these spheres—rhythmic and harmonic—that the New manifested itself most urgently in the works of Stravinsky and Bartók in the first half of this century. Much of what we regard as Stravinsky's most characteristic music is principally rhythmic and harmonic in interest; rhythm, indeed, in *Le Sacre*, say, or *Les Noces*, is promoted to the status of a principle of organization and development (a brilliant feat of emancipation which has been enthusiastically exploited by the *avant-garde*) and there are countless pages in his works of all periods in which the music dissolves into immobile harmony (the chorale which closes the

---

description of neo-classical drama in George Steiner's brilliant *The Death of Tragedy*, London, 1961, p. 19: '... authority and ... reason. Neo-classicism always insists on both. Unity of time and place, moreover, are but instruments toward the principal design, which is unity of action. That is the vital centre of the classic ideal. The tragic creation must proceed with total coherence and economy. There must be no residue of waste emotion, no energy of language or gesture inconsequential to the final effect. Neo-classic drama, where it accomplishes its purpose, is immensely tight-wrought. It is art by privation; an austere, sparse, yet ceremonious structure of language and bearing leading to the solemnities of heroic death.' There is remarkably little friction between the terms of Mr. Steiner's definition and the realities of Stravinsky's music. So close an identification could not have been achieved had the possibility of it not been latent in Stravinsky's genius. His neo-classicism may have been an obligation; but it was also a release.

The New in Rhythm and Harmony

Symphonies of Wind Instruments, for example, the 'bell' chord which consummates *Les Noces*, or the chordal texture of the coda in the finale of the *Symphony in C*; and this feature is not less prominent in the music of his serial phase, whether it be *Movements* or *Threni*). So strong, in fact, was Stravinsky's rhythmic invention and so super-charged with fresh tension his unique harmonic textures that it seemed at one stage as if he had created a valid language from which melody was excluded. One leaves, I think, a performance of *Le Sacre* or *Les Noces* or the *Symphonies* not—to put it crudely, though none the less accurately for that—whistling their non-existent 'tunes' but registering the impact of their rhythm and harmony. Stravinsky, one might think, has written music here which is as consistently and successfully 'about' its rhythm-plus-harmony as a work by Schoenberg is 'about' its melody.

But the composer himself, despite this success, has always been melody-conscious, either consciously circum-venting its absence—demonstrating how well he can manage without it—or consciously filling the gap by reference to melodic models from the past. It is indeed through his melody that the past manifests itself most clearly in Stravinsky's work. To discover an extreme example, extreme because so overt, one needs to seek no further than the final tableau of *Persephone*, where the

[By kind permission of the publishers, Boosey and Hawkes, Ltd.]

serene flow of blandly diatonic melody (Fig. 224) leaves one in no doubt of the composer's conscious affirmation of the past. We may, as so often with Stravinsky, find it difficult to determine *which* past, but we are not left in any

113

doubt that the past is actively involved here in Stravinsky's inspiration.[1]

I have always thought that the two symphonies of his
maturity—the *Symphony in C* and *Symphony in Three
Movements*—offer a succinct, compact summing-up of
essential features of this great composer's art. Both works,
if treated as one unit, remarkably illumine the crisis in
melody which is central to any discussion of his music;
and since Stravinsky's feelings about the past cohere in
their most concentrated form about his melody, any
scrutiny of his melody must bring in its wake a consideration of his neo-classicism (it becomes increasingly clear, I
think, that both the Method and neo-classicism shared a
common interest in keeping melody alive).

The *Symphony in Three Movements* is often described as
one of the most purely Stravinskian of the later works.
Many commentators have sensed in it a 'return' to, or at
least a recrudescence of, the 'old' Stravinsky, i.e., the
composer of dynamic rhythms and emancipated harmonies which are characteristic of *Le Sacre*. The detail of
the comment is not of much interest; it remarks upon the
obvious and neglects the significant achievement which
distinguishes the symphony from the ballet, i.e., the
startling success with which Stravinsky's 'dynamic'
language serves a large-scale symphonic structure. But the
very fact of the response, however inadequately expressed,
emphasizes the singularity of the experience offered by
the symphony. We certainly do not encounter the 'old'
Stravinsky here, since the formal achievement is new. On
the other hand, there is a sense in which the symphony
seems to revert to an earlier stage in Stravinsky's own
music. It is not surprising that ears which had become

---

[1] And Stravinsky's 'present', his own personality, of course, which is made
explicit in the small compass of the melody and its rhythmic build. Though one
immediately, and quite properly, recognizes the reference to the past (this is part
of the intended musical experience) one could never mistake the hand of the
composer.

accustomed to the interest Stravinsky had shown in melody in the 'twenties and 'thirties (*Le Baiser*, the violin concerto, *Persephone*, etc.) were acutely aroused by a work in which melody was conspicuously absent and rhythm and harmony again the dominant components (as in the 'old' days). The jolt was all the more intense since the earlier symphony, the *Symphony in C* (1940), *sustained* the melodic tradition of the previous years as emphatically as the *Symphony in Three Movements* (1945) renounced it.

My suggestion that Stravinsky's neo-classicism is intimately bound up with his melodic practice—that we *hear* his classicism, primarily, as melody—is confirmed, I think, by the response of listeners. Mr. Jeremy Noble, for instance, reviewing a new recording of both symphonies, remarks that the *Symphony in Three Movements* is 'nothing like so "classical" a work as the Symphony in C'; and in the very preceding sentence he himself has observed the striking disparity in the melodic content of both works.[1] By his melody you shall recognize his classicism! Undoubtedly so. But this is to do an injustice to the *Symphony in Three Movements*, which is no less neo-classical, I suggest, than its predecessor; but instead of its classicism, as it were, breaking surface in the shape of defined melody, it is folded within the form, and to that degree is 'concealed' (hence the misconceptions to which the symphony so often gives rise). Is it not the case, in fact, that the *Symphony in Three Movements* belongs to that 'disguised' category of neo-classicism which Stravinsky has discerned as the special type of classicism practised by Schoenberg and his school?

I have said enough, I hope, to show that out of the contrast offered by these two symphonies may grow a better understanding of Stravinsky's use of, or abstention from, melody. In pursuing one aspect of the works one is bound, of course, to exaggerate in order to make one's point. The

---

[1] *The Gramophone*, London, December, 1960, pp. 334–5. I made much the same point in the *Musical Times*, November, 1960, p. 707, when reviewing Vlad's book.

reader will doubtless discover for himself that the more 'classical' of the symphonies is scarcely less rich or characteristic in rhythm and harmony than its partner. As for the *Symphony in Three Movements*, far be it from me to suggest that the absence of melody (the middle movement excepted) is a kind of deprivation. One does not sit listening to it and 'miss' the tunes. On the other hand, it would be positively simple-minded to pretend that one does not notice that there aren't any.

The *Symphony in Three Movements* carries us to 1945. Only three years later Stravinsky was busy with *The Rake's Progress*, the major work which closed, in all essentials, the neo-classical phase of his music. In the 1950s, he embarked on those works (the *Cantata*, *Septet*, the *Shakespeare* songs, *In Memoriam Dylan Thomas*, the *Canticum Sacrum* and *Agon*) which eventually culminated in *Threni* (1957–8), his first wholly twelve-note work. [1]

One stands, in a very real sense, too close in time to the music of Stravinsky's serial phase to write about it with anything like the confidence (misplaced as it may be) with which one approaches his earlier works: they have become part of one's experience, of one's very life, indeed. We need a comparable span of time to assimilate his more recent music. In the case, moreover, of a composer whose powers show no signs of diminishing, whose capacity for adventure seems limitless, one's commentary is bound to be inhibited. One is conscious, always, of the new step that may, as it were, be taken behind one's back and create havoc among one's assessments and predictions. But one must not flinch from the duty to make a judgment out of one's experience of a new work, however immediate it may

---

[1] One should note, however, that in the song-part of the *Dylan Thomas* piece (1954) Stravinsky had already committed himself to a strict application of the Method to his melody. That the row is five-note, not twelve-note, is of less importance, surely, than the comprehensive adoption of the serial principle? We meet here an inspired illustration of a prominent development in the history of the Method: the successful divorce of the serial principle from the obligatory presence of all twelve notes.

be (what else matters in criticism but the spontaneous making of the *right* judgment?). One cannot, inevitably, understand *Threni* as well as one understands the *Symphony of Psalms*. But one knows what one feels about the work, even though it must necessarily remain strange and new for an appreciable period. I should place *Threni*, without reserve, among the grandest of Stravinsky's masterpieces, and am confident that living with the work over the years to come will confirm the good sense of one's instinctive response (perhaps one has 'understood' it after all).

Elating though it is to find that Stravinsky's inspiration is as fresh and rich as ever in the music of what one rashly assumes to be his final phase, one must not be tempted into the appraisal of individual works. The language of music has been our principal consideration throughout this book and it is the extraordinary *fact* of Stravinsky's turn to the Method that demands our continued attention. His adoption of serial practice represents the second of the two great divides that we find in his music (the first was his relinquishment of his Russian 'heritage'): undoubtedly it is the more radical event, since, as Massimo Mila neatly puts it, his works after 1950 show him edging 'closer and closer to the opposite extreme of contemporary musical sensibility of which he was for so long the antithesis'.[1]

I have remarked before upon the fact that Stravinsky's serial phase is the most 'present' of his explorations of the past. He has never before stood so near to an immediate tradition (other than his own). Characteristically, however, it was not until the Method had, in a sense, become an accessible past that Stravinsky's fresh voyage of discovery began. It would be vulgar and trite in the extreme to suppose that it was simply Schoenberg's death in 1951 which prompted Stravinsky to embrace serial technique. The facts of the music, in any case, go against any such

---

[1] Quoted in Vlad, *op. cit.*, p. 178.

pat suggestion of stepping into a dead man's shoes. Stravinsky's serial evolution was swift but not abrupt (he composed himself into the Method, as it were); and gifted with hindsight, as we are at this stage, it is possible to see in certain aspects of his later neo-classical music the gradual unfolding of a new development in his art, though it would have been a bold man who predicted for Stravinsky a serial future.

What is certain is that the Method had already established itself as a 'past' long before the death of its founder, and thus was open, as it were, to negotiation. What is probable, on the other hand, is that Schoenberg's death made a psychological reality of this historical fact; thereafter, Stravinsky was free to submit to his new discipline.[1]

But of the three major Viennese composers who were the essence of the Method's celebrated past, was it not Webern who played the dominant rôle in Stravinsky's serial development? Have we any justification in attributing to Schoenberg a decisive influence?

From what Stravinsky himself has written of Webern, it would seem that acknowledgment of the 'debt' has been made in the clearest terms. 'Webern is for me', he has said, 'the *juste de la musique* and I do not hesitate to shelter myself by the beneficent protection of his not yet canonized art.' In a later volume of his conversations he describes Webern as 'a perpetual Pentecost for all who believe in music'.[2] Schoenberg is not hailed so generously. Stravinsky leaves us in no doubt of his admiration, but his praise is qualified by all the expected—indeed, predictable —reservations. I suspect that he finds in Schoenberg the same 'barrier' that he finds in Berg—a 'radically alien emotional climate'.[3]

It is absolutely true, of course, that Stravinsky's serial

---

[1] See Hans Keller's important essay in Milein Cosman's sketchbook, *Stravinsky at Rehearsal*, London, 1962.

[2] *Conversations*, p. 127; *Memories*, p. 105.

[3] *Conversations*, p. 71.

music sounds not in the least like Berg's or Schoenberg's. But it does not sound like Webern's either, a fact which may strike some as self-evident but, for all that, demands emphasis. It too often happens that what Stravinsky says or writes, about his own music or musical beliefs, is seized upon and quoted as if it were divine law. Worse than that, his music is 'interpreted' in terms of what he writes about it; the work is made to fit the 'explanation'. (No work has suffered more, in this respect, than *The Rake's Progress*. How much has been read, for example, into Stravinsky's incautious reference to *Così*!)[1] I should be the last to deny that Stravinsky's thoughts about his music do not contain the most remarkable and clarifying of insights. But he often changes, or modifies, his opinions (why shouldn't he?) and, more relevant to our present purpose, leaves much *un*said. In any event, the only safe procedure is continuously to check the music against the evidence of the written or spoken statement; when the facts don't match, then it is the music which in a very real sense must have the last word.

If one applies this simple enough test to the music of Stravinsky's serial phase, what emerges most strongly is just what one's experience of all his previous 'love affairs' would lead one to expect: the intensity of his own musical personality. This music is not 'like' Webern, Berg or Schoenberg; it is only 'like' Stravinsky.

There are, it is true, occasional passages in which one's awareness of Stravinsky's interest in Webern is sharpened, in the Passacaglia of the *Septet*, for example, or some minor details of instrumental texture in the later works. But to mistake these 'influences' for a musical affirmation comparable in weight to Stravinsky's verbal appreciation of Webern is to burden the music with a weight which it will not, in fact, bear. The debt to Webern, as distinct from the tribute, remains minor.

---

[1] *Memories*, p. 158.

If this is true of Webern's 'influence', then how much more true it must be of Schoenberg's. But are we sure that the logic of that statement is unassailable? I find, indeed, that it is the very feature which *distinguishes* Stravinsky's music from Webern's that brings it into meaningful relation with Schoenberg's.

'Music', perhaps, is not the right word; 'practice' would be a better choice, a neutral term which emphasizes that what faces us here is not really a matter of style at all, but a question of language. One may readily concede that Stravinsky and Webern have something in common as artistic personalities, that Stravinsky and Schoenberg are radically opposed in just that sense. But as antithetical as these two great composers remain, despite their 'unity' of language, one can point, none the less, to a significant unity of practice which makes a Stravinsky-Webern relation seem merely superficial, dependent on detail rather than substance.

What, in fact, distinguishes Webern from Schoenberg is exactly what distinguishes Stravinsky from Webern: Webern's growing tendency to abandon melody, on the one hand, and on the other, Schoenberg's and Stravinsky's retention of melody as a principal factor in their music. It is in their approach to melody that Stravinsky and Schoenberg present a common front in opposition to the most singular feature, so far-reaching in its consequences, of Webern's compositional practice.

A hint of this (I think) important truth is conveyed by Vlad when he writes of the serial middle movements of the *Canticum Sacrum*, 'On the whole it can be said that while in various instances . . . the instrumentation has a distinct look of one of Webern's scores, the continuity of the vocal line is enough to eliminate any flavour of Webern from the general musical pattern.'[1]

I would agree wholeheartedly with that observation,

---

[1] Vlad, *op. cit.*, p. 194.

but for the words 'continuity of the vocal line' I would substitute 'melody' (why fear to use an old-fashioned but strictly relevant term?). Can it be denied, indeed, that Stravinsky's serial music is peculiarly rich in melody? Both the *Canticum Sacrum* and even more recent cantata, *A Sermon, A Narrative and A Prayer*, are rich in melodic content; but richest of all, perhaps, is *Threni*, which proliferates melody on a scale exceptional by any standards, and most exceptionally so by Stravinsky's own. He sustains his melodic invention until the very end of the work, until the closing pages of the 'De Elegia Quinta', when, with a gesture characteristic of his genius, he dissolves his melody into harmony, and in so doing writes one of the most beautiful of his many resolutions imagined as a predominantly chordal texture.

It is, of course, important to remind ourselves just who characteristic Stravinsky's genius remains in his serial phase. Yet we risk overlooking the most remarkable feature of his serial music if we blindly concentrate upon what is self-evidently characteristic about it. It is not surprising, I think, that it is again his melodic invention which makes an urgent claim on our attention. I have suggested above that the Method, for Stravinsky, was already a 'past' before he turned to it; and he does no more than run true to his own form in making this past, too, immediately recognizable in melodic terms. But what is surely exceptional—indeed, *un*characteristic—is the richness and extent and strongly personal contours of his serial melody?[1] The fund of melody we find in his most

---

[1] An exception to this is *Movements*, of course, one of the toughest of Stravinsky's serial pieces, and tough because the melodic dimension is not pronounced. But though the work in this respect may appear to be uncharacteristic of his serial music, it remains characteristic of his work viewed as a whole. As we have seen, he has often written music in which rhythm and harmonic texture are the principal factors. *Movements* is true to this tradition. In any event, if this style were to be reexplored in serial terms, it was bound to happen in an instrumental composition. That the bulk of Stravinsky's serial music is vocal in conception inevitably makes melody a central issue. *The Flood*, in its vocal numbers, sustains the flow of

recent music is, I think, something new in his art; new in its extensiveness and new in its independence of a discernible model. Because, although the Method is, in some sense, a model for Stravinsky, it imposes, as I have remarked before, no condition of style upon those who use it as a language. Hence his serial melody is free of the interplay between *two* creative personalities which is part of the fascination we so often find in the melody of his neoclassical period. The Method, in fact, has made possible for Stravinsky a development of the very quality that his own 'past', in some sense, may be said to have lacked: a strong melodic gift that owes its life exclusively to his own inspiration.

---

melody, while its instrumental numbers (i.e., the ballets, especially the 'Building of the Ark') exploit other spheres of invention. It is interesting to note that for his depiction of the Flood itself Stravinsky returns to the ostinato technique of earlier days, but now the repetition principle is applied to a row.

IV

POSTSCRIPT (1963)

Vlad writes that 'the main problem, on the solution of which the very survival of music as a coherent form of aesthetic expression would seem to depend, is to restore to music the unity of language it had lost as a result of the post-Romantic dilemma'.[1]

If my book has a theme at all, it is just that situation which Vlad describes; and Stravinsky's late serial music provides me with a strictly thematic finale that is composed of notes, not words. His adoption of the Method, with which the wheel of history turns a full revolution, would seem to assert and affirm that very 'unity of language' which Vlad, in my view, rightly stresses as the 'main problem' of our time.

'Unity', as we have seen, has been dispersed among various 'means of continuation'—nationalism, neo-classicism and the Method. It is striking, however, how much history, in each case, is bound up with the problem of melody. One scarcely exaggerates, in fact, if one claims that music in the first half of this century is also the history of the fortunes—and misfortunes—of melody.

This preoccupation with melody lends unity even to the contending schools, a unity of creative interest and principle that bridges the gaps between the discrepant styles, though it does nothing to diminish their width. It is, as I have suggested, the tenacious interest of Schoenberg and Stravinsky in melody that unexpectedly introduces an

---

[1] Vlad, *op. cit.*, p. 176.

element of unity into their serial practice; in a sense, a unity more musically significant than any offered by the fact of both composers exploring a common language. ('Common', in a serial context, means as much, or as little, as the use of 'common' to describe the linguistic unity of Haydn and Mozart. It is to compositional practice *within* a given language that we must look for evidence of real affinities and contrasts.)

A natural and happy consequence of Schoenberg's and Stravinsky's, in general, steadfast adherence to melody, has been the exclusion of abstraction as a trend in their composing. It was the Method, above all, which opened up the vista of abstraction in music (Cubism performed the same service for the visual arts); but, though abstraction was latent in the Method, and developed by one of Schoenberg's own pupils, there was never a serious danger that Schoenberg himself would succumb. He was too heavily committed to the regeneration of melody. His music had to have a 'theme' in every sense of the word.

Likewise Stravinsky, who, in his serial music (with the possible exception of *Movements*), has shown no tendency to go 'abstract' on us. As for the works of his neo-classical and Russian periods, we have seen how melody-conscious they are, even those in which melody, as it were, plays the rôle of an absentee-landlord and thus necessitates the presence of compensatory ruling agents.[1]

Our two composers' treatment of melody may be very different—Schoenberg's characteristically developmental, Stravinsky's characteristically static—but their music leaves us in no doubt that, for them, melody has retained its status as an 'object'. It is thus that abstraction is kept at bay.

I have mentioned more than once the complementary

---

[1] It may be objected that I attempt to have it both ways, and so I do. I do not, however, claim it as *my* prerogative, but as the prerogative of genius; and it is exactly this which confronts us in those curious cases of Stravinsky's 'missing' melody (see pp. 112–13).

character of Schoenberg's and Stravinsky's approaches to the New. Their serial music, while presenting us, exceptionally, with a genuine affinity of practice in the melodic sphere, sustains the tradition of complementation. Stravinsky, for example, kept tonality dynamically, if idiosyncratically, alive while Schoenberg was as rigorously exorcizing it. But Schoenberg, in some of his later serial music, once again came to grips with tonality. This was not a return to functional tonality—not even a reconciliation of tonal with serial practice—but a readmittance of certain tonal features as part of the serial organization. Tonality is admitted, as it were, on serial terms.

The development of Stravinsky's serial music, however, has run a different course, the curve of which neatly complements Schoenberg's. His first steps towards, or in, the Method juxtapose both tonal and serial principles of organization; at the same time, the serial inspirations themselves are often tonally orientated ('The intervals of my series are attracted by tonality; I compose vertically and that is, in one sense at least, to compose tonally. . . . I hear harmonically, of course, and I compose in the same way I always have.').[1] It is significant that *Threni*, Stravinsky's first wholly twelve-note composition, is also integrally tonal. (In *Threni*, the composer writes, 'simple triadic references occur in every bar',[2] a feature of the work he describes on another occasion as 'a kind of triadic atonality'.)[3]

Despite the contrasts in individual harmonic practice, both Schoenberg's later and Stravinsky's earlier serial music presents a 'triadic atonality' (a useful term, this) which has been reached by paths not so much parallel as directly opposed. Perhaps this is more an affinity and less a complement? The line between the two, in any event, is a thin one.

---

[1] *Conversations*, pp. 24–5. [2] *Memories*, p. 107.
[3] *Expositions*, p. 107.

A Unity of Language

What counts is the remarkable synthesis[1] that both composers have achieved by such very different means, a synthesis typical, one may think, of the late-period manner one would expect a Schoenberg or Stravinsky to show.

It would seem, in fact, that this very synthesis offers the 'unity of language' to which Vlad refers. One cannot, of course, be sure that the kind of reconciliation that Stravinsky has effected between tonality and the Method will remain a permanent feature of his work. He surprised himself by composing the anti-tonal *Movements* (1959). Who knows what surprises are yet to come? On the other hand, his more recent cantata, *A Sermon, A Narrative and A Prayer* (1961) clearly sustains the pro-tonal character of *Threni* (1958) and so does his dramatic Biblical Allegory, *The Flood* (1962). If he continues, as seems likely, with his present exploration of the forms dependent upon vocal or choral forces, whether a new cantata or new work for the musical theatre, it is more than probable that it is the tonal and melodic aspects of Stravinsky's serial technique that will engage our attention.

But though one may concede that Schoenberg and Stravinsky, between them, have restored to music the possibility of a unified language, one has to wonder, in 1962, whether this noble achievement does not mark the close of a period rather than herald the birth of a new. For the New in music today is largely based on attitudes and practices which consciously reject what one had innocently imagined to be the stepping-stones to the future laboriously laid down by Schoenberg and Stravinsky. Melody,

---

[1] Stravinsky, of course, especially in his neo-classical music, has often proved himself to be a great synthesist of past and present. He has sustained the rôle in some of the music out of which his serial phase emerged, not only in his masterly juxtaposition of tonal and serial procedures but in the reconciliation of his own past with his evolving 'present'. *Agon*, for instance, though it looks forward, also looks back quite explicitly to Stravinsky's characteristic neo-classicism. This remarkable work, in fact, brings under one roof two of the mainstream movements of the first half of our century, neo-classicism and dodecaphony, a notable synthesis by any standards.

in particular, the preservation of which I have suggested was one of the main concerns of composers in the first half of this century, has been abandoned. It is too early, as yet, to attempt any singling out of a feature that may lend unity to the present array—or disarray—of compositional practices. But if they are united in little else, it is in their often rancorous opposition to the concept of melody (and everything that goes with it) that the leading composers of the new generation share common ground. One wonders nowadays if any aspiring composer would risk his reputation by committing himself to anything as solecistic as a good tune.

Ten years ago it seemed probable that music was entering upon a phase of pure abstraction fathered by Webern, whose purity, indeed, one may applaud while still holding in reserve the gravest doubts of the 'weight' of his undeniable genius. Does he not remain a very small composer, despite the size of his influence? But, of course, historically speaking, what counts here is the size of the influence, not the size of the talent. It is wise to remember, none the less, that what a composer is taken to be by his successors is an inevitably uncertain instrument of evaluation; he may prove to have been greater or smaller than his influence.

None the less, in the 1950s few would have countered the claim that Webern rather than Schoenberg was to be the key-figure in an evolving serial future, that it was Webern who opened up new means of serial practice which had been neglected (or simply ignored, or even not noticed) by the more traditional and conservative-minded Schoenberg.[1] Webern's innovatory athematicism and Stravinsky's emancipated rhythmic structures—these were the two main streams which were to fertilize the subsequent decade.

---

[1] I think the *formal* predicament of younger composers at this century's halfway point was a real one, perhaps as pressing as the problem of style or language at the century's beginning. One can sympathize with the disappointment they felt at Schoenberg's disinclination to follow up the radically unorthodox forms of some of his earlier music without necessarily recognizing the validity of their own 'radical' solutions of the formal problem.

Total Serialization

But if a pattern of development, however abstract, were discernible in the 1950s, no such easily identifiable situation seems to exist in the 1960s. One kind of New, indeed, already seems to have given way to another, or if not entirely supplanted, at least to have been deeply infiltrated by the doctrines of another, in some sense, radically opposed 'school'.

It is not, perhaps, surprising that the period of 'total serialization', a fanatical extension and intensification of principles deduced from Webern's works, would appear to have been only short-lived. The strict post-Webernites seem to me to have offered a classic illustration of jettisoning the baby along with the bath water. Melody and its resources, for so long a guarantee of comprehensibility and prime vehicle of communication, were renounced, and to fill the gap, one might think by way of wellnigh guilt-laden compensation, composers subjected their material to manic disciplines of serial systematization, the inaudibility of which was often as total as their organization. Never was music so over-determined, and never so difficult to *hear* as an expression of order in terms of sound. Boulez' *Structures*, one assumes (because one has not succeeded in experiencing their organization as *sound*), are 'about' nothing other than their structures. But even the most open and admiring ear (one recognizes the brilliance of Boulez' musical personality) is baffled in performance by the absence of audible sequence or logic. The ear yearns for a structure upon which it might lean. It is one of the paradoxes of recent musical history that invention so rigorously systematized should make so unsystematic an impression. One craves, in a sense, for more system, not less.

Composers now seem to have abandoned their efforts to achieve intelligibility through total serial organization. What, creatively, may have been gleaned from this intransigeant experiment, what new extensions (or modifications?) of serial principles may yet be unfolded, only the future will reveal.

It is indeed ironical that if the listener's problems were only intensified by the vigour of the post-war plunge into determinacy, the later (and widespread) eruption of *in*-determinacy has done little or nothing to bring him relief. One would be rash to venture a suggested anatomy for music in the years since 1950, but it already seems clear that a prominent feature of the period will prove to have been this extraordinary swing from the wholly determined to the wholly indeterminate, a swing which also covers a great deal of middle ground in which mingle compositional practices fertilized by both extremes. It seems no less clear, at the moment at least, that the achievements of electronic music (another region in which predetermination looms large) remain minor. Pure electronic 'music' still sounds most convincing when most 'like' music. As for *musique concrète*, its material never began to sound sufficiently unlike itself, and thus never began to approximate to a condition of either 'music' or music.[1] But

---

[1] In his *Lecture on Electronic and Instrumental Music* (*Die Reihe, Reports/ Analyses*, London, 1961, p. 62), Stockhausen states that 'one can recognize a first criterion for the quality of an electronic composition by hearing the degree to which it is free from all instrumental or other auditive associations. Such associations divert the listener's comprehension from the self-evidence of the sound-world presented to him because he thinks of bells, organs, birds or faucets.' If judged by this criterion, it is not surprising that *musique concrète*—which has so often seemed chained to the familiar, self-evident sound-world of the bathroom geyser—should be found wanting. Stockhausen continues: 'From this we should conclude that it is best for electronic music just to sound like electronic music, that is, that it should as far as possible contain only sounds and sound-connections which are unique and free of association and which make us feel we have never heard them before.' But, though this pure, ideal electronic 'music' can be—and is —manufactured, the non-computed ear still tends to listen to it as music (not 'music'). One cannot escape one's auditive inheritance, and one's ear, however battered, however emancipated, brings assumptions and associations to an electronic session which, willynilly, inflect one's response. What seems nearest to music, is what one finds, relatively speaking, intelligible. This seems to me to be a virtually unbreakable vicious circle. One is faced by a game, the rules of which one can never hope to learn, unless, that is, one can grow a pair of virgin ears, un-contaminated by the past. (The same problem, surely, faces the *composer* of electronic music. May we not attribute at least some of his lapses from pure electronic grace to an inner ear still conditioned by the instrumental sound-worlds

whether the music is random, computed, predetermined, or a mixture of current 'schools', the listener is likely to find all of it aurally baffling, because object-less, from every point of view. (One may note here that if some post-serial developments correspond to the abstraction that succeeded Cubism, the current trend of random composition has its parallels with tachisme.) In earlier days, a listener might ask quite properly and not unmusically what a work was 'about'; and expect to be answered by a demonstration, without recourse to extra-musical terms of reference, of a reality that was strictly audible. (Mr. Hans Keller's Functional Analysis, nothing if not an ideally audible demonstration, provides one type of convincing answer to the listener's question.) But much of the newest of the new music is not open to analysis, to investigation, of this kind; not open, even, to the question that has prompted analysis in the past. At one (random) extreme it is intendedly, and successfully, 'about' nothing; at another, it is 'about' itself, a statement with an honourable pedigree in the history of music (cf. Stravinsky's oft-quoted thoughts on the subject), but given a new twist in our time.

In the past, 'music "about" itself' has also meant, without any implication of reduced integrity, music about music; the most radical composers never wholly lost touch with the language of their predecessors, even when they were criticizing it. We have seen, indeed, how the two great radical masters of the first half of this century, Schoenberg and Stravinsky, guaranteed a basis for continued comprehensibility, for continued communication, by holding fast to practices which might still be meaningfully related to 'tradition' (tradition in the sense of an accumulated

---

of the past?) If, as electronic composers suggest, electronic 'music' is to coexist with 'conventional' instrumental music (though conventional, of course, is to be taken in their sense of the term), then it seems that two pairs of ears—one for 'music', the other for music—will become obligatory; not to speak of two kinds of concert halls.

experience of the past, against which, inescapably, we listen to, and compose, our music), 'critical' of tradition—calcified tradition—though their innovations were.

'The artist cannot start from scratch but he can criticize his forerunners.' This is the point, perhaps, to reintroduce the 'motto' with which my book opened, in the shadow of which, in fact, it has been written. What is asserted there by Professor Gombrich, and most brilliantly and convincingly argued in his *Art and Illusion*,[1] is surely relevant to music, and never more so than at the present time when composers seem bent on achieving the opposite of what he claims: starting from scratch and not so much criticizing their forerunners as totally rejecting them. Of course, if one wholly abandons an established, inherited vocabulary, music which is self-evidently 'about' itself is, at last, made a reality. But it is a reality which, by excluding the possibility of association and verification, also excludes the possibility of communication. The composer becomes his own—and only—audience.

It could be the case, undoubtedly, that music will change its fundamental nature. Because it has been one thing, one has no right to assume that it will never be another. Perhaps music will, after all, become 'music'. But there is no way of foretelling the way in which music may yet evolve. What could be more surprising, more explicitly out of historical true, than the prospect of Britten, in the second half of this century, filling the rôle of a—perhaps the—major European composer? One might think it both a welcome prospect and a proper tribute to the size of his genius. His language, none the less, has been left fundamentally untouched by the most radical of the innovations whose development we have traced in the earlier parts of this book (which is not to say that his own language has not developed radically across the years). If history were our sole guide, we should be obliged to look

---

[1] London, 1960, p. 321.

to other horizons for a major figure. But presented with
the *fait accompli* of genius, history must take second place,
though, as it happens, it *is* the curious history of English
music which has played a not inconsiderable part in the
shaping of Britten's genius. It is a strange but undeniable
fact that a time-lag seems to operate, whereby English
composers often come late—and fresh—to a language that
elsewhere may already have grown tired. How else can one
explain the astonishing feat of Elgar, for example, who
wrote two splendid late-romantic symphonies which were
more 'late' in chronology than in actual style? The tradition of romantic symphony could be freshly handled by
an Elgar, who approached an old European tradition as a
newcomer and out of his English 'innocence' wrote symphonies in the spirit of Schumann and Brahms which
magically avoid anachronism. What one instinctively
recognizes as the romantic tradition of symphony dawned
later in England than anywhere else. Through the re-
generative power of Elgar's genius, it was lent, out of time,
a new lease of life.[1]

This 'out of time-ness' is, of course, much less marked in
Britten's case than in Elgar's. I have no doubt, however,
that the vitality of his language owes something to his
urgent exploration of European models, a discovery which
had been unnaturally delayed—and thus made all the
more pressing—by an intervening period when English
composers were obsessed by the necessity (real or imagined)
to establish an 'English' convention. The impact of
Mahler, of Berg, of some Stravinsky, was all the more
intense, and all the more intensely felt, because this was
ground which had remained, hitherto, a closed, alien
territory to the English composer. An almost dramatic
sense of stylistic release informs the best of Britten's
'European' music. In recent years, he has tended to re-
discover his English past, but in a spirit free of archaism.

---

[1] I have argued this point of view in greater detail in 'Some Thoughts on Elgar
(1857–1934)', *Music and Letters*, Vol. 38, No. 2, April, 1957, pp. 113–23.

The Choice Today

Indeed, in some ways, Britten's discovery of 'his' past may be compared to Stravinsky's.[1] Does he not make Purcell, for example, accessible to new feeling? It seems probable that the past will always provide a legitimate source of creative stimulation in just this sense. Neoclassicism, indeed, in its widest application, may still have a future.

One cannot predict the course events will take, least of all the influence of genius, known or as yet undeclared, upon the 'laws' of history. The choice today would seem not to be between serial or non-serial (an exhausted conflict) but between comprehensibility and incomprehensibility. It is the very concept of music as a language which is now in the balance.

---

[1] In his *Flood*, by the way, Stravinsky seems to have 'discovered' Britten. His twin-voice conception of God (baritone and bass) clearly has its origins in the contralto-tenor combination which Britten devised for the same purpose in his Canticle II, *Abraham and Isaac*, and used again in his Canticle III, *Still falls the rain*, but this time combining tenor and horn. Stravinsky's *Abraham and Isaac*, incidentally, goes a long way to confirming the extraordinary melodic fertility of his late serial period (see pp. 120–2). 'Unending melody' may yet prove to take on a peculiarly Stravinskian relevance, if this work is anything to go by.

V

CROSS-CURRENTS
WITH EXPRESSIONISM

It is extraordinary how the anxiety to pursue one idea can result in the suppression of other ideas, equally relevant. Thus it astonishes and shames me that in the Index to the first edition of this book, there was no entry for Expressionism. The term, indeed, let alone the important movement with which the term is associated, found no place on any page.

This, it strikes me now, was a pretty memorable omission in a book that pretended to survey the relationships between the arts in the first half of this century, but it was only one reviewer—among the many who thought the book 'stimulating' (a word I came to dread)—who spotted my lapse, Mr. O. W. Neighbour, in *Music and Letters*.[1] He wrote, quite properly, of my failure 'to mention Kandinsky', and pointed out, again with strict relevance, that 'Schoenberg was, of course, closely associated with Kandinsky, and the common ground between their aesthetic ideals is perceptible in their work at this crucial period'. The common ground was Expressionism.

It will be clear enough to the reader who recalls the argument of the book to this point that it was my preoccupation with Cubism which led me to neglect Expressionism, but I would emphasize that it was not an omission made, as it were, at the expense of Expressionism. If I can now give the movement its rightful place in my perspective, I

---

[1] Vol. 44, No. 22, April, 1963, pp. 184–6.

think that it will prove to offer a parallel that complements the parallel I have drawn between Cubism and the Method. (It will not, I believe, replace it or contradict it.) On the whole, I stick to my guns, or to my parallels, rather. Though they have been sharply criticized, it remains my conviction that they make a valid and even illuminating point: that the arts, if not quite the whole, then at least a significant part of the whole, moved towards abstraction; and that out of the efforts of leading artists to retain a mode of communication among increasingly incommunicative techniques, two languages evolved, the Method and Cubism, which, in intention and influence, showed some remarkable features in common. This still seems to me to have been worth saying.

Mr. Neighbour was right to pick me up when I incautiously state (on p. 89) that 'abstract art could never have happened *without* Cubism'; right, because Kandinsky, an Expressionist, was in fact the first 'to venture into the new realm of abstract painting'. 'It was Kandinsky who realized the idea and who produced the first abstract paintings that are artistic wholes.'[1] Though it seems not possible to establish an exact date for the first abstract painting, we can safely attribute the discovery of the idea to the period 1908–1912 and to Kandinsky himself.[2]

---

[1] H. K. Röthel, *Kandinsky: the Road to Abstraction*, Marlborough Fine Art Ltd., London, 1961.

[2] Sir Herbert Read interestingly documents the event in his essay on Kandinsky (Faber Gallery, London, 1959, pp. 3–4), where he also valuably points out (pp. 2–3) that the seeds of abstraction were already latent in *Art Nouveau* or *Jugendstil*: '. . . there came a point when abstraction *as such* was deducible from the extremes of Jugendstil, and the discovery was Kandinsky's.' Music, too, might be said to have had its *Art Nouveau* or *Jugendstil* group of composers, those senior figures— Reger, Debussy, Strauss, Mahler, for example—whose styles, however various, clearly showed the kind of friction between late romanticism and the emerging New that is characteristic of the parallel groups in painting and architecture: hence my earlier reference to Charles Rennie Mackintosh (p. 78, n. 2). It can certainly be no accident that our immediate present has suddenly discovered the importance of *Art Nouveau*. 'In my end is my beginning.' Small wonder that having come to one sort of cultural end in our time we should look back to the beginning of it all.

Schoenberg and Kandinsky

(There is an *Abstract Composition* by Kandinsky, dated 1912.)

As Mr. Neighbour points out, the association between Schoenberg and Kandinsky (1866–1944) was a close one, how close can be verified by any reader who cares to turn to Schoenberg's published letters, a volume which contains a wholly remarkable document addressed to the painter.[1] We also learn from it an exceptionally interesting and still perhaps too little known fact, that Kandinsky, who, from 1922 to 1933, was on the staff of the Bauhaus, pressed Schoenberg to join the institution which, in so many ways, and in so many departments of the arts, was the breeding-ground of the New in the first decades of the twentieth century. Schoenberg, super-sensitive to intimations of anti-semitism, declined the offer;[2] but the offer, for all that, was immensely significant and revealing of the generally and unusually collaborative feeling between artists in every sphere during this period of creative ferment.

There is, after all, the fact of Schoenberg's own remarkable accomplishment as a painter, those extraordinary portraits and visions[3] which form part of the history of the Expressionist movement in painting: three works by Schoenberg, indeed, were included in the first exhibition organized at Munich (1911) by the *Blaue Reiter* group of artists, of which Schoenberg was a member. Sir Herbert Read reminds us of Kandinsky's preoccupation with music, and anyone who reads Kandinsky's book, *Concern-*

---

[1] See also p. 139, n. 1.

[2] *Arnold Schoenberg Letters*, London. 1964, pp. 88–93, and particularly p. 88, n. 1. One wonders, too, if Schoenberg *had* joined the Bauhaus staff whether or no a book would have come out of the association, as was the case with Kandinsky and Klee.

[3] Some of Schoenberg's paintings are reproduced in Josef Rufer, *The Works of Arnold Schoenberg*, London, 1962. As Kandinsky himself remarks (see p. 137, n. 4), Schoenberg's paintings fall into two styles: intuitive, imaginary portraits ('visions') on the one hand, and on the other, paintings 'from' Nature.

ing the Spiritual in Art,[1] in which Schoenberg's *Harmonie-lehre* is quoted and Schoenberg himself enthusiastically mentioned, must be struck by the conviction with which Kandinsky held his belief that painting aspires to the condition of music. Musicians cannot but feel at home in a text that makes such liberal use of musical metaphor, and not only metaphor (e.g., rhythmic, melodic, symphonic) but strictly musical terms (e.g., fermata). Kandinsky's 'Improvisations'—his own title for a particular type of often non-representational painting—can certainly be understood in a musical sense. Kandinsky described these as 'spontaneous expressions of incidents of an inner character, or impressions of the "inner nature"';[2] and elsewhere he writes that 'Inner necessity is the basis of both small and great problems in paintings. Today we are seeking the road which is to lead us away from the external to the internal basis.'[3] Indeed, throughout his book there is much talk of 'inner necessity', a phrase that has an authentically Schoenbergian ring about it. In Kandinsky's own essay on Schoenberg's paintings, he speaks of them as the subjective expression of an inner impression,[4] a description that might well apply to some of Schoenberg's non-tonal music.[5] When we read Kandinsky, it is surprising how often the tone of voice reminds us of his great contemporary.

It is always the case when reading Schoenberg on music that one is struck by his lofty conception of the art and his concern—like Kandinsky's—with the spiritual, a concern that is distinctly out of fashion these days but was of the first importance to Schoenberg. It was in fact a concern

---

[1] *Über das Geistige in der Kunst*, Munich, 1912. There has been more than one English translation. I have made use of Hilla Rebay's—*On the Spiritual in Art*, New York, 1946.

[2] P. 98 of the translation referred to in n. 1 above.

[3] Quoted in B. S. Myers, *Expressionism*, London, 1963, p. 166.

[4] In a symposium, *Arnold Schoenberg*, Munich, 1912, pp. 59–64.

[5] Sec pp. 28–36.

with the spiritual that was a distinguishing feature of the *Blaue Reiter* group as a whole and marked them off from the *Brücke* group, the other main but very different body of Expressionist painters.[1] As Dr. Röthel has it, '. . . the *Blaue Reiter* artists gained, through the speculative efforts of Kandinsky and the religious ethos of Franz Marc, a certain spiritual quality foreign to the other group. The *Brücke* followers did not talk, they painted. Their works are like an outcry. The members of the *Blaue Reiter*, however, started from the intellect, they analysed, philosophized. They were just as much interested in religious questions as in the developments in modern music, in the theatre, and in literature.'[2] This was a circle to which Schoenberg belonged with absolute ease—it represented, as we can see for ourselves, the extraordinarily wide range of his own personality and interests. It is not surprising that in later years Kandinsky recalled Schoenberg's enthusiastic support of the *Blaue Reiter* idea. We can also assume, I think, that Schoenberg greatly contributed to it, as Sir Herbert Read seems to recognize: 'Kandinsky's aesthetics (a total aesthetics covering all the arts) stands or falls by the justness of this [musical] analogy, and from the early days of the Blaue Reiter it was based on discussions with composers like Arnold Schoenberg.'[3]

---

[1] Another, highly significant difference was this: that whereas the members of the *Brücke* group were often brutally naturalistic in manner and gloomy in tone, the *Blaue Reiter* artists were not only frequently playful in spirit but increasingly non-representational in style (e.g., Kandinsky and Klee). 'The road to abstraction' was travelled, in the main, by artists from the *Blaue Reiter* group, not from the *Brücke*. (See also p. 150, n. 1.)

[2] H. K. Röthel, introduction to the catalogue of the *Blaue Reiter* exhibition at Edinburgh, 1960.

[3] Read, *op. cit.*, p. 7. This just assessment does not, alas, prevent Sir Herbert from developing a misleading parallel between Kandinsky's aesthetics and Stravinsky's. 'There is, I believe,' he writes, 'a close similarity between the formal evolution of these two great contemporary artists.' I believe, on the contrary, that this view can only be held if one discounts the experience of Stravinsky's music, which seems to me to represent a world quite alien to Kandinsky's. With Schoenberg, on the other hand, there are parallels both aesthetic and strictly musical. If there were not, they would not be worth talking about.

Musical Analogy

Music certainly played an important rôle in the first and, as it turned out, only issue of the almanac associated with the group: *Der Blaue Reiter*, published in Munich in 1912. There were not only articles about music, among them Schoenberg's 'Das Verhältnis zum Text' (which many years later was included in *Style and Idea* (1951) as 'The Relationship to the Text') and an essay by Leonid Sabanayev on Scriabin's *Prometheus*,[1] but also an extensive musical supplement, comprising a reproduction of the MS. of Schoenberg's *Herzgewächse*, a song by Berg (op. 2, no. 4) and a George song by Webern, 'Ihr tratet zu dem herde. . . .' Schoenberg, who was clearly responsible for the choice of music, was also represented by two paintings, his *Selfportrait* and *Vision*.[2]

I have mentioned earlier Kandinsky's emphasis on 'inner necessity'. The phrase turns up again at the end of one of his most eloquent statements of his favourite musical analogy: 'colour is the keyboard, the eyes are the hammers, the soul is the piano with many strings. The artist is the hand that plays, touching one key or another purposively, to create vibrations in the soul. It is evident therefore that colour harmony must rest ultimately on purposive playing upon the human soul; this is one of the guiding principles of internal necessity.'[3]

---

[1] The fact that the *Blaue Reiter* almanac singled out Scriabin for attention is of itself a fact of some interest. There can be little doubt that Scriabin's attempted association of music and colour must have fascinated those Expressionists who were, so to say, looking at the problem from the other side of the fence. Kandinsky actually conceived a colour organ, 'which projected colour images on a screen in response to keyboard manipulation' (B. S. Myers, *op. cit.*, p. 168). There is surely a link here with the fantastic 'Colour Scene' in Schoenberg's *Glückliche Hand*, for a cinematic version of which he suggested Kandinsky as a possible designer of the main scenes (See *Arnold Schoenberg Letters*, *op. cit.*, p. 44). As Robert Craft wittily observes in his notes that accompany Vol. I of the gramophone records devoted to Schoenberg's works (Philips), *Die glückliche Hand*, with its exact coordination of colour and music, is among 'the first operas of the age of electricity in which the application of electricity is actually composed'.

[2] *Selfportrait* is reproduced in Rufer, *op. cit.*, Plate V.

[3] Quoted in Myers, *op. cit.*, p. 167. Miss Dore Ashton (see p. 148, n. 1), the American art critic, writes interestingly (p. 199 of her book) about the significance

Mr. Bernard S. Myers, in his study of Expressionism, underlines the 'lyrical spontaneity', the 'otherworldliness' of artists like Kandinsky and Klee, qualities which are certainly conspicuous in the passage I have just quoted; and he continues to speak of the *Blaue Reiter* group's 'fundamental reliance upon intuition, upon the heart rather than the intelligence. Their spontaneity, especially that of Kandinsky and Klee, would seem to be tied up with a reliance on subconscious motivation, on the kind of automatic compulsion that would affect the abstract Surrealists. . . .'[1]

Sir Herbert Read reminds us that Kandinsky was not very precise in his definition of 'inner necessity'—'he seems to have regarded it as an indefinite spiritual (or one can say psychological, or even neural) tension which was released in the act or process of composition. There is no doubt that he always had the analogy of musical composition in mind. . . .'[2]

But whatever vagueness may surround the term 'inner necessity', there can be little doubt that in Kandinsky's whole approach to painting, to the development of his new style, we find a close parallel with Schoenberg's musical development in the same years. Kandinsky, having abandoned the object (though this was not an immediate process but a gradual dissolution, as it was also for the Cubists), having embarked on his new style, the 'road to abstraction', was obliged to rely on spontaneity, on intuition—the dictates of 'inner necessity'—to see him through. There being no grammar, as it were, to help him

---

of 'no colour' for Kandinsky, who related white to 'the silences in music' in these remarkably prophetic words: 'White . . . acts upon our psyche as a great, absolute silence like the pauses in music that temporarily break the melody. It is not a dead silence but one pregnant with possibilities.' Miss Ashton points out that the 'silences and intervals imagined by Kandinsky have assumed great importance in contemporary painting'—and also, one feels bound to add, in contemporary music. Webern, certainly, would have known what Kandinsky had in mind.

[1] Myers, *op. cit.*, p. 159.
[2] Read, *op. cit.*, p. 6.

out, because this new style was the start, for him, of a new language, he had no option but to trust to his inspiration or, if you prefer it, his Unconscious.

I have written at some length in the first chapter of this book of Schoenberg's 'historic plunge into the Unconscious'[1] and have no wish to weary the reader by repeating the arguments here. But Kandinsky, whom I neglected to mention before, must also take an honourable place among those twentieth-century artists who were Schoenberg's collaborators in opening up new realms of feeling; and it is his intimate association with the composer, the similarity and interaction of their aesthetic beliefs in the crucial years under survey (from 1908, or thereabouts, to 1916), and the emergence of kindred (to put it no stronger than that) principles of creative practice in an almost identical creative situation—it is these considerations that promote the title of this chapter, 'Cross-currents with Expressionism'.

It was Schoenberg (though it might well have been Kandinsky, one feels) who wrote, 'One must be convinced of the infallibility of one's own fantasy and one must believe in one's own inspiration',[2] words which, in the context of Schoenberg's non-tonal music, i.e., the music preceding his discovery of the serial Method,[3] reflect what Mr. Myers rightly isolates as the leading features of the *Blaue Reiter* school of Expressionists: a 'fundamental reliance upon intuition . . . a reliance on subconscious motivation . . .'. It was this precarious spontaneity which had to serve in place of a rule.

Schoenberg, likewise, having relinquished tonality, found that he had to rely on *his* intuition, on 'inner necessity', to lend unity and coherence to his 'free' compositions in the absence of that 'subconsciously function-

---

[1] See pp. 38–51.

[2] *Style and Idea*, p. 106.

[3] A period discussed on pp. 28–36.

ing *sense of form*'[1] which composers had acquired from tonality; and the result, though certainly not wholly abstract in character in the sense which I deplore earlier in this book,[2] was certainly *more* abstract, i.e., athematic in trend, than the music of his later, serial period, when the Method, or so I have argued, acted as a positive bulwark *against* abstraction, for which reason, indeed, I suggest that the Method was, in part, evolved.[3]

But Schoenberg's own dissatisfaction with the potentialities of a 'free', non-tonal style, I have already documented. What remains clearly to be stated is this: that Schoenberg's non-tonal period can quite properly be thought of, and described, as Expressionist in character; that he not only contributed to this immensely important movement, but substantially influenced the shaping of its doctrine; that there was a genuine parallel in technique between composer and artist, if that is the right word for so purely intuitive a creative approach; and finally, that Expressionism in both painting and music opened up the road to abstraction. If Kandinsky was the first to paint an abstract composition, Schoenberg, no less, was the first to explore similar possibilities for music.

If nothing else, this brief examination of Schoenberg's re-

---

[1] *Style and Idea*, p. 106.

[2] See, in particular, pp. 90–2.

[3] Mr. Robert Craft, in his notes that accompany the recording of *Erwartung* (see also p. 139, n. 1), scorns those who describe the work as 'a-tonal, a-thematic, a-harmonic, and so forth', and continues: ' *Erwartung* is almost purely "thematic", as well as perfectly "tonal" and perfectly "harmonic" . . .' I am not quite sure in what sense Mr. Craft uses these terms, but it seems to me that they would have to be much qualified if they were to retain any meaning in the context of Schoenberg's (in my view) non-tonal or a-harmonic music. Would Mr. Craft suggest, for example, that, say, 'thematic' and 'tonal', as we understand them in relation to Schoenberg's early (tonal) music, are meaningful in the same way when it is *Erwartung* or the Five Pieces for Orchestra, op. 16, that we are discussing? Or that 'thematic', as we understand it in relation to Schoenberg's serial phase— when it remains, as it happens, meaningful in the traditional sense—can be used of his pre-serial, i.e., non-tonal, music without qualification? A dubious proposition, I should have thought, and one that surely runs counter to the evidence of the music itself.

lation to Expressionism usefully, because I think accurately, defines a whole period in Schoenberg's career. He has, of course, been liberally associated with Expressionism by other writers (many of them taking a hostile standpoint), but the term has too often been used in a blanket sense, without discrimination among periods or types of work.

When Schoenberg moved on from his non-tonal phase, he left Expressionism behind him; and though what one might care to consider Expressionist traits crop up now and again in his later music, his departure from the *Blaue Reiter* aesthetic was decisive. Readers who have stayed the course as far as this will not need to be reminded that Schoenberg's attempted renovation of the language of music through the Method, his re-assembly of a vocabulary, a grammar, for music, encouraged me to develop in Chapter II some thoughts on the common ground shared by the Method and Cubism. Kandinsky himself points out that 'Almost in a day (1911–12) two great styles of painting came into the world: Cubism and Abstract (=Absolute)[1] painting. At the same time Futurism, Dadaism, and the soon triumphant Expressionism were born. These were hectic times!' Hectic times, indeed; but that the first steps towards Cubism and the first abstract painting (not to speak of like developments in music) all emerged in so narrow a space only goes to support the view of Giedion's that has so often been quoted in these pages: the common 'emotional background' of all creative minds in whatever sphere that gives a period not only a unity of feeling but a certain unity of practice in techniques and modes of expression. It is not surprising, for example, that the *Blaue Reiter* artists 'instinctively sensed something of the significance of the scientific revolution.'[2]

Kandinsky, naturally enough, speaks of Cubism and Abstract painting, his own innovation, as if they were

[1] This is not an equation that satisfies me, time-honoured though it may be. See p. 91, for my suggested clarification of it, so far as music is concerned.
[2] H. K. Röthel, Edinburgh catalogue, pp. 6 and 23 (see n. 2, p. 138).

comparable movements. But important though Kandinsky's break-through was, and as important as his own work was in itself, there can be no doubt that it was Cubism which proved to have the wider influence, not only on artists but on countless aspects of everyday life; there is good reason, in fact, for thinking of Cubism as the 'parent of all abstract art forms',[1] even if the thought is, as it were, bad history.

Cubism, I have suggested earlier, came to dominate the scene because it contained within it the seeds of a possible language for painting. It is surely of interest that Kandinsky in later years attempted to rationalize his Abstract painting into a 'total aesthetics', to create a grammar of painting; and that his own later compositions (though it is not established that he was influenced by the Russian Suprematists and Constructivists) developed a geometric vocabulary that was seized upon by his imitators. In Kandinsky, too, in fact, we seem to encounter the drive to create a language, an effort to escape an art that works by intuition alone.[2] Schoenberg's great contemporary moved on from his first abstract period, as did the composer from his non-tonal works, possibly under the same kind of creative pressures and with the same objective in view.

These general considerations of Schoenberg's relationship to *Blaue Reiter* Expressionism—a group which, Mr. Myers interestingly suggests, played an important rôle as

---

[1] See p. 90.

[2] In some respects, Kandinsky's rationalization of what was essentially intuitive shows features in common with the development of Cubism, which was also a rationalization of spontaneous acts of creation: in both cases, and inevitably so, imitators accumulated along with the rationalizations (you can imitate a rationalization but not an intuition). But whereas, as Kandinsky observed, Cubism and Abstract painting were born almost simultaneously, it was Cubism which established its language, its vocabulary, the more swiftly, and hence, of course, enjoyed the more immediate influence. By the time Kandinsky's 'total aesthetics' had evolved, Cubism in any strict sense was past its climax. On the other hand, it is a latter-day Expressionism, if anything, that is now prominent in music and painting. One cannot help noticing how the fortunes of the Method and Cubism have followed remarkably similar historical patterns.

What is Expressionist Music?

'a link between the analytical propensities of the French school and the more emotional and intuitive interests of the Germans'[1] (Cubism was to make its mark on more than one leading member of the group)—leave untouched whole areas of essential, indeed, crucial, detail.

Has anyone attempted, for example, to define Expressionism in music, isolating, that is, a specific sound by which Expressionism manifests itself?[2] Expressionism is certainly used widely as a descriptive term, and more often than not so loosely that it is difficult to attach a peculiar meaning to it. There is an obvious field for research here. If Strauss's *Salome*, Berg's *Wozzeck*, Busoni's *Doktor Faust* Shostakovich's *The Nose*, Bartók's *The Miraculous Mandarin*, Schoenberg's *Erwartung* and *Die glückliche Hand* all have something in common[3]—I choose my examples from the operas and ballets that were performed at the 1964 Florence Maggio Musicale, when Expressionism was the subject around which the festival was built—what on earth is it? What, in short, distinguishes Expressionist music from other music?

I do not wish to appear to dodge this exacting question, but even to try to answer it in detail would hopelessly outrun the scope of this small book. However, if I were ever to embark on an exploration of this kind, I should certainly follow up a remark of Schoenberg's on his own non-tonal music, when he conceded that, though 'much was lost', 'new colourful harmony was offered'. And there,

---

[1] Myers, *op. cit.*, p. 164.

[2] I am not forgetting Luigi Rognoni's *Espressionismo e dodecafonia* (Turin, 1954), which surveys much of the field that I touch on here. But as the title of his book suggests, Mr. Rognoni proposes a closer relationship between Expressionism and the Method than I would accept. For me, as I argue in this chapter, it is the pre-serial period of Schoenberg that can be described as strictly Expressionist in character. The Method represents a different and later stage in his development, though I would agree that a residue of Expressionist traits remains.

[3] No doubt everyone could make their own additions from works by Prokofiev, Schreker and even Puccini, whose *Girl of the Golden West* strikes me as showing some interesting Expressionist features, particularly in its harmonic style.

I think, we find at least the beginning of a fruitful approach to this question of Expressionism in music. For is it not true that it is primarily through the emancipation, volume and density[1] of its harmonic gestures that music makes known its Expressionist character?[2] Through rhythm, too, of course, which brings works like Bartók's *Miraculous Mandarin* and even Stravinsky's *Sacre* within the orbit of Expressionism (these works, also, on the grounds of density and volume!). But melody less so, I should have thought.[3] It is almost always harmony that has the upper hand, which is exactly what I would expect of music from this period of turbulent innovation: as I have argued elsewhere, harmony, in our century, has tended to develop at the expense of melody, and Expressionism, inescapably of its time, was bound up with that momentous development.

But 'volume' and 'density'? I introduce these words (perhaps they are ill-chosen) because it seems to me to be vital to make some possible and valid distinction here between Impressionism (in music) and Expressionism. The distinction is clear enough in painting—as Mr Myers has it, the Impressionist approach is 'a description of

---

[1] Density more often than not, but sometimes just volume and one note, e.g., the blood-curdling unison on *B* in Berg's *Wozzeck*, which must be the most celebrated Expressionist crescendo in the history of music.

[2] There is a particularly interesting remark of Schoenberg's in this connection. When writing about a projected cinematic version of *Glückliche Hand* (see p. 139, n. 1), he suggested that the film 'should have the effect (not of a dream) but of *chords*' [my italics]. The analogy is striking.

[3] Nevertheless, we can in fact speak quite properly of 'Expressionist melody', because melody in this period, and particularly Schoenbergian melody, developed those wide leaps that are a distinctive Expressionist feature. This was a stylistic trait that survived the Expressionist years and influenced in no small measure the character of twentieth-century melody. As so often, we find in Mahler, a prophetic genius if there ever was one, frequent intimations of Expressionism. In the Adagio of the tenth symphony, for example, the wide leaps of the main tune foreshadow the characteristic contours of Expressionist melody (the line between *extreme expressiveness* and Expressionism is a very thin one), while the famous piled-up dissonance in the same movement (just before the coda) is another typical Expressionist gesture, but this time harmonic, not melodic.

something tangible', the Expressionist, 'the graphic representation of a mood'[1]—but blurred in music, since harmony predominates as the instrument of expression in either case. Yet we do not, on the whole, mistake an Impressionist composer for an Expressionist. Why not?

This is where density and volume may come in handy. For I think there is a real difference in the degree of 'release' that we find in Impressionism and Expressionism. The latter, surely, was the art of release, *par excellence*, in which the composer or painter wanted his inner experience, that 'inner necessity', to strike home without, so to speak, passing through the usual channels of communication. The experience, so conveyed, *is* the work of art in its totality. In Impressionism, on the other hand, much more an art of suppression and deliberate inhibition, a more formal organization, to be consciously perceived, is still part of the experience. The nakedness of the experience is mitigated, as it is not in Expressionism, by conventions and assumptions that form part of the traditional language of music,[2] the language spoken between composer and audience.

---

[1] Myers, *op. cit.*, p. 172. We must also remember that Impressionism helped to make Expressionism possible, in the sense that the tonal instability introduced by Impressionism, as Schoenberg himself points out in *Style and Idea* (p. 104), facilitated the 'emancipation of the dissonance' which is a characteristic feature of Expressionism.

[2] In the main, of course, tonality, which, though often suspended or exiguous in Impressionism, is rarely negated, as it can be in Expressionsim. On the other hand, there is no *absolute* tonal *v.* non-tonal distinction to be made between Impressionism and Expressionism in music. Many composers touched, at least, by Expressionism (e.g., Strauss, Prokofiev, Shostakovich, Bartók) were basically tonal in style: Schoenberg's consistently non-tonal Expressionism presents an almost solitary example of stylistic purity. Still, I don't know that one would go far wrong in suggesting that Expressionist manifestations, more often than not, resulted in music that strained tonality to its extreme limits. And it is in this sense, perhaps, that Expressionism, which was combatively anti-Impressionist in spirit (the paradox was that Impressionism assisted at the birth of this hostile progeny), stands in clear contrast to the parent movement. But as so often with movements in the arts, we meet not just wheels within wheels, but a complete revolution of the cycle. Might it not be argued, for instance, that both Impressionism and Expressionism have a common 'parent' in Wagner? Debussy, after all, owed a

All this is doubtless clumsily put, but it remains true, I think, that whereas in Impressionist music we expect, and meet, harmonic invention in which dissonance is muted, however acute, an often low level of dynamics (think of the reticence of Debussy's *Pelléas et Mélisande*) and transparent textures, in Expressionism we move into a world of sound that presents a reverse situation: heavy, dense (which is not to say impenetrable) textures, an often high level of dynamics (certainly extreme contrasts in dynamic range) and harmonic invention charged, well-nigh explosively so, with explicit tension (i.e., a high rate of dissonance). Whereas Impressionism permits the listener some degree of objectivity in his rôle, Expressionism, in its own remarkable way, involves the listener in the sound it makes, not quite by deafening him, but certainly by pushing to the limits of the tolerable the magic power of maximum volume.[1]

great deal to him; and Expressionism could scarcely have happened without Impressionism, for all its anti-Impressionist assertions. The old cliché—i.e., the comparison of the differences between French Impressionism and German Expressionism—really needs rethinking in the light of a common source. No doubt national characteristics may have had something to do with both trends— rational, analytic France and impulsive, introspective Germany—but much more interesting is the multiple rôle played by Wagner in the unfolding of twentieth-century developments. His shadow grows the longer, the more one studies him.

[1] Wagner, astonishing genius that he was, often seems to me to have had a foot in both the Impressionist and Expressionist camps. If he could be the most delicate of composers, he could also be the most overwhelming in terms of sheer physical impact of sound. Perhaps I also ought to add that it is clear that many of the 'sound-events' of the present-day *avant-garde* have their origins in Expressionism. As M. Antoine Goléa suggests, for example, in his article in the *Musical Quarterly*, Vol. LI, No. I, January, 1965, p. 31: 'Boulez's style in all his works is that of the most violent Expressionism. . . . This music, this technique, in the hands of an authentic composer, is a cry from the depths, the unanimous protest of our age against the overwhelming cruelty of our condition.' Indeed, the more one looks back into the history of the arts in the twentieth century, the more one is struck by the precedents that can be uncovered for many of the seemingly novel departures that we have witnessed in our own day. While writing this very note, a new book has come to my attention, *The Unknown Shore: A View of Contemporary Art*, London, 1964, by Dore Ashton, which includes an intelligent and perceptive assessment of the very real relationship between *avant-garde* music and *avant-garde* art ('Music and Painting', pp. 197–211). Miss Ashton quotes John Cage:

There are doubtless many reasons why Expressionism, as a general movement in the arts, has seemed to enjoy a reputation for dealing in—dealing out—painful emotions. I notice in a recent article, for example, that Mr. Ronald Stevenson congratulates Alan Bush on having avoided in his Berlin years 'the spiritually poisonous and rancorously pessimistic influence of Expressionism.'[1]

This would not be a point worth taking up, were it not for the fact that it represents a fairly widely held view of the movement.[2] I find it irritating because it seems to me to be both superficial and imprecise as a judgment. It would be positively simple-minded not to concede, when one surveys the Expressionist field, a conspicuous preoccupation with violence, the grotesque, the pathological, and nightmare events.[3] Furthermore, it is arguable, at the least, that this art of release became ultimately too dependent on the personal constitutions of the artists concerned and confined in scope for that reason.

But to hold informed reservations about the nature of Expressionism is not to fall into the trap of imagining that every Expressionist sprang fully-armed from Dr. Caligari's famous cabinet (it would be interesting to discover how strong has been the influence of the visual images of the cinema on most people's conception of the Expressionist movement). It is, moreover, plainly inadequate to write

---

'When starting to be abstract, artists referred to musical practices to show that what they were doing was valid, so nowadays, musicians, to explain what they are doing, say "See, the painters and sculptors have been doing it for quite some time".' This thought, in my view, represents a confusion between the concepts of the abstract and the absolute. But a confusion, alas, can be as influential in its way as an insight. Miss Ashton also points out that 'abstract Expressionism', a term first applied to Kandinsky's improvisations, was revived in 1946 to describe the 'informal' painting that emerged in America (pp. 192–3). Expressionism, in fact, is still with us, in both music and painting, if scarcely in manifestations that the founders of the movement would wish to recognize.

[1] *The Music Review*, Vol. XXV, No. 4, November, 1964, p. 326.

[2] See pp. 51–2.

[3] But would the Greek dramatists emerge unscathed by criticism based on norms of moral health? How hygienic, for that matter, is *Hamlet*?

about Expressionism without reference to the practice and stated beliefs of its leading exponent. For there can be no doubt about it, the charge of 'rancorous pessimism' simply does not stick so far as Kandinsky's art and expressed aesthetic doctrine are concerned. Quite the contrary: he was, as Miss Ashton emphasizes, a 'romantic idealist'—'It was his belief, nourished by a nineteenth-century background, that man was the better for art, and could, in fact, help shape the destiny of mankind through his art. Nothing could be less marked by irony than his optimistic treatise *Concerning the Spiritual in Art*.'[1] And if Kandinsky's treatise was optimistic, his art was elating, and often gay in spirit.

Expressionism undoubtedly had its dark side, and there is no denying that it was often painful, disturbing feelings that broke surface in this art of release. But no judgment of the movement can be taken seriously that neglects to assess all the strands of counterpoint that go to make up the total texture.

Schoenberg, though he had his own vein of musical humour, was not a composer that one would describe as naturally light of heart. But if, in Expressionism, as seems to be the case, we can distinguish between optimistic-idealistic and pessimistic currents, there can be little doubt as to which trend Schoenberg belongs. 'Romantic idealist', as for Kandinsky, would serve him as a by no means unworthy epitaph.

---

[1] Ashton, *op. cit.*, p. 191. The optimism of Kandinsky and his circle was in strong contrast to the generally depressed atmosphere of the *Brücke* group of Expressionists. A social pessimism was indeed a marked feature of their work. I wonder again if Expressionism as a term has not become too closely identified with the brutal naturalism of these artists, to the exclusion of the idealism of the *Blaue Reiter*.

VI

POSTLUDE (1965)

The musical scene since 1963 (when this book was first published) has shown nothing like the succession of radical events that left their mark on the immediate post-war decades. Stravinsky, as Leavis once said of Eliot, has 'gone on', with a handful of new works that seem to consolidate rather than extend his late style. Britten, too, has gone on, with a series of works, *War Requiem* (1961) and Cello Symphony (1963) prominent among them, in which his rare and highly complex sensibility (never more so than in the spectacular coda of the Cello Symphony's finale) continues to inform whatever medium he cares to select. *Curlew River* (1964) marks a fresh departure, in that this audacious church 'opera' reveals a freedom of rhythmic counterpoint (*not* random in principle, as has already been wrongly suggested, but precisely calculated in extent, degree and effect) that is certainly new in his music; demanding, indeed, its own system of notation. It is typical of the composer that this new development[1] is unfolded in a work which outwardly, at least, is bound up with the prehistory of the musical theatre.

---

[1] New, yes. Nonetheless, there are significant precedents for the freedom of *Curlew River*, some of them in unlikely places, e.g., the conversational recitative-ensembles of *Albert Herring*. Another signpost is surely the remarkable prose (narrative) style Britten adopted for some of the Owen settings in his *War Requiem*. The *Songs and Proverbs of William Blake* (1965) suggests that the influence of *Curlew River* on Britten's composing is likely to be profound.

As for the senior members of the *avant-garde*, Boulez and Stockhausen, while their presence is still felt, it is noticeable that it is their past reputations rather than their new works which continue to reverberate. Stockhausen has not now made an impression with a new piece for some time.[1] Perhaps tireless experimentation—and certainly something of the laboratory atmosphere hangs about this enigmatic figure—has replaced the act of creation. Boulez, though patently the more musical of the two and less of the engineer—his recent success as a conductor has only made explicit that intense musicality which many of us sensed in his compositions, even the most formidable of them—has also not proved to be prodigal of music, at least not of completed works. More often than not it is a fragment, part of some work in progress, that is revealed. There is always the promise of a major piece, rarely the fulfilment of it.[2] Composing, when all is said and done, ultimately must depend on compositions, not on conducting, on lecture-tours—or expectations. Boulez will not be the first composer in the history of the art who has found composing difficult. But it is perhaps a symptom of the curious impasse which music has reached today that the difficulty experienced by audiences with new music is matched, ironically, by the difficulty some 'difficult' composers have in composing. The growing recognition of the genius, peculiar but real, of Olivier Messiaen has been a welcome feature of the past two or three years, but it would scarcely have been possible if there had not been a

---

[1] *Carré* (1960), for four orchestras and choruses, is perhaps the most recent work of Stockhausen's to have aroused widespread interest and comment, though it has not enjoyed anything like the *succès d'estime* of the earlier *Gruppen* (1958).

[2] The painfully slow materialization and assembly of the composite, five-part *Pli selon pli, hommage à Mallarmé*, is an example. M. Goléa (see n. 1, p. 148) confirms my own thoughts about Boulez: 'The disturbing fact is that for the past three years, if one excepts a short fragment presented at Basel in January 1964, Boulez has produced nothing, even though, in compensation, he has directed [i.e., conducted] more and more'.

quantity of music awaiting recognition.[1] The same might be said of that very distinguished and substantial American composer, Mr. Elliott Carter.

Fertility, of course, is not all; but it is something. It is, for a start, an unmistakable aspect of Hans Werner Henze's composing of which one has to take note; and when it is joined, as it is, to a highly topical and accessible style, it is perhaps time to wonder whether or no this remarkably talented musician has not achieved the synthesis which would effectively bridge the gap between the 'modern' composer and his audience. That Henze has, to some extent, succeeded, cannot be doubted: his popularity speaks for itself. But the quality, the significance, of his success seems to me to remain open to doubt.

Henze's eclecticisim is legendary, and a recent work, his cantata, *Novae de infinito laudes* (1961), poses the problem of derivativeness in an acute form: the work presents, in a very appealing form, a kind of anthology of Stravinskian manners, from the *Symphony of Psalms* to *Threni*. And yet the derivations are far from straightforward, which is where the problem intrudes. On the contrary, Henze has a genuine capacity to lyricize the monumental, reduce the epic to human scale and introduce warmth into austere ritual. The transformation is often beautiful; but the final effect is conspicuously diminishing. One senses at the heart of this prodigious talent a secret ambition to take the sting out of 'modern' music.

This type of synthesis, I predict, will not prove to break the impasse, the communication-barrier. A policy of appeasement, though immediately attractive and pacifying, leaves the basic problem untouched. One prefers, perhaps perversely, the uncompromising, unrelenting and humourless posture of the *avant-garde*. Their music, if

---

[1] A recognition that is certainly not confined to an appreciation of the historic rôle played by his second étude for piano, *Mode de valeurs et d'intensités* (1949), in the development of new music since 1945, major document though that work is.

only in a negative sense, has at least made us think afresh, and think urgently, about the very nature and function of music. They have questioned, possibly valuably, and certainly insistently, assumptions about the art inherited from the past that had become unthinkingly accepted as aesthetic dogma; and it may well be that their reassessment of the materials of music, of sound—not to speak of their unconventional excavation of instruments—will ultimately extend the repertory of expressiveness. What the *avant-garde* needs above all, as I have argued elsewhere, is a composer. Perhaps the future will bring us one, who will at last musicalize, and make fruitful, the often barren experimental harvest of his predecessors.

At one stage, it seemed not altogether impossible that the actual course of music, and its established character, might be altered by the concerted efforts of the *avant-garde*: music, one feared, might become 'music'. But it seems to me that that particular danger is passed, that at the time of writing a space for breathing and taking stock prevails. If this is so, it is, surely, because the *avant-garde* simply have not written the works which might have consolidated their position. And after all, in any kind of revolution, it is deeds, not words, that count. The *avant-garde* have certainly not given us a short measure of words: but their works have flowed far less generously.

I should make it clear, of course, that by *avant-garde* I mean those few radical composers who have to be taken seriously: we don't have to worry about the rest, however sensational, and however much newsprint their sensations consume. It is a curious fact, I think—and perhaps a sign of the generally confused standards of the times—that some contemporary music, and some of the least reputable at that, only achieves a 'serious' status through being written about, and discussed, in journals of opinion. The notices that the works receive bestow upon them the wholly undeserved importance of an 'event': it is one of the great weaknesses of criticism that it tends to treat everything as of equal importance and is obliged to use the same language for both the trivial and the significant. An example comes to hand in the pages of a respected American journal, the *Musical Quarterly*,[1] where Mr. Udo Kasemets reports from Ann Arbor. Excerpts from his chronicle—it is *not* a parody—run as follows (the italics, titles apart, are mine):

. . . the opening composition of the festival [was] Donald Scavarda's *Landscape Journey*. It is scored for clarinet, piano and two film projectors. Its form resembles a simple rondo where the A sections are built of slowly moving sound-patterns whereas the B segments are represented by a soundless visual play of fast-moving colours and shapes on two screens. The sounds, too, emphasize colour. The clarinet part consists of multiple harmonics, complex overtone and undertone clusters, windless key-tappings, pitchless airflow through the instrument, and so on. The pianist plays on the keyboard, on the strings, produces muted sounds, harmonics, unusual resonances. The combined effect of the tender, eerie sounds and the restless, somewhat aggressive colours on the screens is haunting, *yet utterly sensitive and memorable. It is a very intellectual score, but in it lies uncommon beauty and delicacy.*

George Cacioppo's *The Advance of the Fungi* is possibly less intellectual in concept, but its sound-qualities, though utterly different, are as intricate and imaginative as those of the Scavarda work. Here a male chorus, three clarinets, two horns, three trombones, and percussion produce colours that can rarely be associated with any of those normally heard from ensembles of similar makeup. . . . There is nothing gimmicky in the use of these unorthodox vocal and instrumental techniques. *They are employed with logic, consistency, transparency, economy, and, most of all, with great aural sensitivity and obvious musicality. The result is a score that moves and impresses.*

[Gordon] Mumma's *Megaton for William Burroughs* [is] an electronic composition, conceived for 'live' concert performance. Five performers manipulate four to six channels of taped source material and two to four channels of amplified sounds produced with various objects (such as a piece of wood-and-wire sculpture, a reconstructed and specially prepared upright piano, assorted pieces of

---

[1] Vol. L, No. 4, October, 1964, pp. 515–19. I am indebted to author and journal for permission to quote so liberally from this article.

metal, wood, and plastic). . . . Here electronic music has been liberated from its laboratory straitjacket and brought back into the realm of spontaneous music-making. *It is a work of prophetic vision and artistic grandeur.*

Robert Ashley was represented by two works: a symphony, *in memoriam Crazy Horse*, and an opera, *in memoriam Kit Carson.* . . . For the festival performance Ashley had recruited eight couples who were seated in a circle surrounding small tables carrying a portable radio, a television set, and a phonograph. The players' actions were essentially those associated with any conventional, civilized [sic] party: repetitious superficial conversation, exclamation of stock platitudes, people turning on and off radios, TV, and phonographs, name-dropping, laughter, coughing, hand-clapping, bored yawning, and so forth. It was amazing to see how the logical organization of Ashley's score rules these nonsensical actions with such a rigid hand that out of the apparent chaos emerged a performance that had both an explicit meaning and an esthetically pleasing shape. The opera emerged at once as a satire on social habits and emptiness *and as a musical score (though not a single musical sound was uttered)* that moved in cautious, well balanced steps from a vigorous 'tutti' towards a lulling 'morendo' ending, so well in keeping with the social comment the performance aimed to bring into focus. It was *musical theatre at its most intense*, audio-visual-theatrical 'pop art' in its most refined form. *But most of all, it was a work of a composer who has brought a new order of simplicity into the world of up-to-date music.* . .

Mr. Kasemets' chronicle certainly makes lively and surprising reading. Surprising, too, is the language in which he formulates his judgments: 'musical theatre at its most intense'; 'a work of prophetic grandeur and vision'; 'a score that moves and impresses'; 'utterly sensitive and memorable'; 'uncommon beauty and delicacy'; 'logic, consistency, transparency, economy, . . . great aural sensitivity and obvious musicality'; and so on. Honest, enthusiastic reactions, no doubt; but there would seem to me to be an alarming gap between the expectations of musical masterpieces aroused by Mr. Kasemets and the character of the works he writes about ('not a single musical sound was uttered', as he tells us himself, in Mr. Ashley's opera). It would be impertinent of me to question Mr. Kasemets' judgments, all the more so since I have not had the opportunity of experiencing the works themselves. What I do question, however, is the appropriateness of his language. Is it meaningful, in short, to attempt to convey to us the experience of Mumma's *Megaton for William Burroughs* in the same terms that we would normally reserve for, say, Beethoven's Ninth—'a work of prophetic vision and artistic grandeur'?

Perhaps Mr. Kasemets is himself aware of the linguistic problems. I notice that he writes, when opening the last paragraph of his chronicle: 'Of new works of more "human" character heard during the festival, . . .'

I wish I could assume that those quotation marks round 'human' were ironic.

VII

MUSIC OR 'MUSIC'? (1968)

Whither the New music? Only the most complicated of answers is possible, but one fact at least can be concisely stated: the New music is no longer created or performed in those places where we looked for the old. Ernst Krenek, himself a composer of the senior generation (whose music is too little known these days), moderately and intelligently states the case in the collection of essays, *Exploring Music*, which has recently appeared in an English translation. In an essay entitled 'On the Ageing and Obsolescence of Music'—surely a neo-Schoenbergian title which reflects the Old Master's 'New Music, Outmoded Music, Style and Idea'?—he writes:

... most performances of new music take place in an atmosphere dominated by specialists—composers, critics, musicologists, students, musical executive organs, conductors and the like. In the main, however, these specialists do not go to an art-work for a total emotional experience; they are interested in the demonstration of new materials, new principles of composition, procedures, methods. The broader application of such achievements to a large number of subjects worth writing and presenting interests them less than the unique experimental demonstration of the invention. This creates the danger of a radicalisation that will accelerate continuously, ending in a sad cul-de-sac where perhaps even the unique experiment will hardly be worthwhile because it can already be considered out of date before it has even happened.[1]

Krenek was writing in 1956 but was already sensitive to

---

[1] *Exploring Music*, London, 1966, p. 225.

what one might describe as a radical shift in intention and location. Music, especially in the United States and Europe (but now England is catching up, if that's the right phrase), has moved substantially into the university and the laboratory, and communication—or at least the intention to communicate—is no longer the baton that every aspiring composer carries in his knapsack. On the contrary, communication as we have known it in the past, when the artist has not thought it dishonourable to 'speak' to his audience or cultivate a 'voice' of his own, has been downgraded or completely abandoned. In 1968 we seem to be locked in the cul-de-sac that Krenek anticipated. It is surely significant that a prominent part of Stravinsky's recent advice to a young composer (delivered in *The New York Review of Books*) was a reminder that he should *compose*—

that is, not strive for Foundation awards, academic prizes, college presidencies, foreign fellowships; not attend culture congresses, not give interviews, not prattle on the radio about music appreciation, not review new scores (except his own, pseudonymously); and not, either insidiously or directly, push, promote, manoeuver, advertise, finagle, operate.[1]

One notices that the great composer does not expressly state in his timely catechism that the young composer should seek an audience, but perhaps we have no right to expect that unambiguous opinion from someone who has always claimed to have written to please himself and 'the hypothetical other'. On the other hand, in pleasing himself Stravinsky has also managed to please a vast number of people at the same time, so for him the problem scarcely exists. Was it, in any case, ever a problem for most of the composers that we regard as great? One needs no convincing that Mozart too wrote as much for himself as for a specific audience. But can we doubt that part of his acknowledged greatness rests in the miraculous capacity, characteristic of the majority of great artists, to speak,

---

[1] *The New York Review of Books*, issue of June 1st, 1967.

however intimately and subtly, to a very large public? We
live in an age dominated by the slogan of 'mass communi-
cations' but tend to forget that the art of mass communication has been practised by the major creator in advance
of the theories of Marshall McLuhan.

To communicate, in whatever medium, we have to
'speak'; and if, as one suspects, and as has been persua-
sively argued in other quarters, the very language of
music is in a state of flux, small wonder that the current
musical scene presents such confusing features at almost
every level. As Stravinsky again has written:

I could not begin to distinguish music and non-music in some of the
concert-hall activity I have observed of late, nor would I be confident
of recognizing a new musical genius. In fact, if I were asked to fill
Schumann's role today, and hail a new Brahms, I would probably
have to modify his dictum to: 'Keep your hats on, gentlemen, for all
I know he may be a charlatan.'[1]

Stravinsky, of course, is noted for the excellence of his
wit and the elegance of his malice, but he makes two very
serious points. How do we begin to evaluate the New
music on the one hand, and on the other, how do we discriminate between music and 'music'? (Never did inverted
commas bear such an interpretative weight.) The last
question poses in a nutshell the peculiar predicament we
face today, a crisis for which it is difficult, perhaps impossible, to look to the past for means of solution. Suppose,
for an unlikely moment, that it was Haydn who was being
questioned about his young contemporaries. His judgment
of rising genius (though the very concept would doubtless
have been strange to him) might have been wrong, because
great composers are often, and for good reasons, uncertain
critics. The established genius (a much more insecure
creature than most people imagine) is rarely generous or
illuminating about the emerging talent who may prove to
be a rival. We have seen this clearly enough in the case of
Stravinsky himself who has welcomed many a swan in one

---

[1] *Ibid.*

volume of his conversation books only to dismiss him as a goose (or a dead duck?) in the next: the carnage, indeed, is impressive and impressively varied—Boulez, Britten, Messiaen and Xenakis are only a few of the composers who have suffered the razor's edge of Stravinsky's tongue. Haydn would doubtless have been more polite, more *galant*, but he could have committed the same kind of misjudgment, hearing everyone else's music through a pair of ears that, understandably, had a prejudice in favour of his own. Whereas Stravinsky, however, confesses that he now has no guide-lines by which to discriminate between the genuine and the bogus, Haydn, despite his prejudices (if any), could have summoned to his aid a whole grammar of music which at the very least would have enabled him to discern the competent and reject the faulty or sub-standard product, an instrument of evaluation which brings us up hard against Stravinsky's dilemma. For if in Haydn's day there was only music or *bad* music, in our time there is music, 'music' and non-music; and though we may still think that we recognize music when we hear it—works, that is, that still retain some audible link with tradition—we are hideously at sea when confronted with the extremer manifestations of the *avant-garde*, not just because we are all fossils or otherwise moribund, but because we seem to—no, we do—find it well-nigh impossible to make any rational judgment at all; and when the possibility of judgment is removed, whether positive or adverse, confusion pours in to fill the vacuum.

The sceptic may object, of course, that all this is a case of history repeating itself. Have we not already lived, he may ask, through the very same barrage of protestations, cries of despair and prophecies of catastrophe in the past, and the recent past at that, except that then it was composers like Schoenberg, Berg, Bartók and Stravinsky who were classed as unintelligible and chastised for undermining the art of music? And one has to admit that, yes, the modern movement in music was abused in much the same terms that we express our discontent with the practitioners of today's New music. But does it follow, therefore, that just as the major figures in the modern movement have, on the whole, won acceptance on a broad front, today's *avant-garde*, in due time, will achieve similar recognition? In short, is it all a matter of time, of perspective, before we clasp to our bosoms a March, fully comprehended even though 'Composed and realized by two computers in liaison together'? (The title is genuine, not invented.)

Such optimism is illusory. The passage of time brings many surprises, it is true, but in fact, if we regard time past in strict relation to the modern movement, the surprise it offers in the way of altered perspective scarcely encourages us to view the relation between tradition and the New in the arts as a perpetual race between a tortoise and a hare. One thing, indeed, musical developments since the Second World War have made absolutely and ironically clear: that all the battles fought on behalf of the modern movement in music—the struggle to gain Schoenberg a hearing, to secure Stravinsky a place as someone other than the composer of *Firebird* and *Petroushka*—were fought under the wrong banner. We all thought at the time that our efforts to promote the modern masters of the day were not only designed to achieve recognition for music of genius but also to guarantee a future—a new future—for the art itself. The modern movement, if only it could be established, was the promise of a new dawn.

From our present vantage point everything looks very different and perhaps slightly disillusioning. The new dawn has turned out to be a sunset, or if not that, then certainly a summit tinged by the rays of a traditional sun. For instead of the modern movement carrying us forward into a new period, the leaders of it now emerge as grand old men magnificently chipping away at the old, familiar veins from which their predecessors had mined their materials. As the years roll by, in fact, what seemed to divide the most significant and influential composers—Schoenberg's serial method, Stravinsky's brand of neo-classicism or Hindemith's—seems of little importance if compared with the central ambition which united them: the determination to extend and above all to maintain the great tradition into which they were born.

This radical revision of our approach to the history of twentieth-century music has not yet found its way into the text-books, and, without it, what we read is necessarily misleading and muddled. All too often, in the absence of a real perspective we have as substitute a mass of detail—flitting from composer to composer, from style to style, from school to school—which finally strikes one as hugely irrelevant and totally unilluminating. Professor William W. Austin's large-scale study, *Music in the 20th Century*,[1] is a painful case of not seeing the wood for the trees. It would be ungenerous to suggest that he has not collected some valuable facts or written some modestly perceptive pages about those composers he best understands. But he is defeated at every turn by his laborious attempt to achieve comprehensiveness, a task which is well beyond the capacity of one man. One man in fact simply can't know enough.

To list all the oddities that catch the eye in Professor Austin's book would take almost as many pages as he spends himself on 'Further Steps in France, Italy, England' or 'Composers Comparable to Prokofiev' or 'Successors to Prokofiev' (the chapter titles are wholly revealing). For example, Mr. Hans Keller is solemnly listed as one of 'several distinguished refugees' who brought to England in the 1930s 'a variety of styles incorporating something from Schoenberg' (along with Wellesz, Gerhard, Seiber and others). Mr. Keller's merits are indeed outstanding—how one wishes he might be persuaded to write a book about twentieth-century music—but he

---

[1] New York and London, 1966.

would surely be astonished to find himself established as a *composer* of influence. Odder still, Roberto Gerhard, who might be thought to have made a not insubstantial contribution to the contemporary scene, receives no further musical attention at all, whereas an entirely minor German figure like Joseph Haas is given thirty lines which read—though this may be an uncharitable assumption— as if they were a paraphrase of a handout from the Haas Society of Munich. Tippett fares no better (no thirty lines for *him*), whereas Gerald Finzi, another minor talent, does quite as well as Haas. On the other hand, when one comes to grips with what Professor Austin has to say about Finzi, perhaps it comes as a relief that Tippett (among many others) has been spared. The quality of the comment is scarcely encouraging: 'A less known English composer, Gerald Finzi (1901–56), concentrated on songs and choral music in a style more personal than Walton's, more refined and more conservative, obviously related to Parry, Elgar, Holst, and Vaughan Williams, and not so obviously but nevertheless deeply affected by Byrd, Dowland, and Purcell.'

Never were so many big names dropped in so small a space about so slight a composer! A pedigree so general in tone, so replete with Influences and Comparisons, does not lead us to savour whatever distinctive voice the composer may have had; and the absence of genuine perspective and discrimination—Arthur Bliss, a much more substantial figure than Finzi, one might think, receives no more than a bare mention—is finally crippling. Professor Austin has laboured vastly but largely in vain.

Yet another Comprehensive Survey appears in the shape of a reissue in hard covers of the fiftieth anniversary number (1965) of *The Musical Quarterly* (New York), a collection of essays devoted to *Contemporary Music in Europe*.[1] Here again the pursuit of comprehensiveness

---

[1] New York, 1965, and London, 1966.

undermines the strength of the enterprise, though it is an advantage to have imposed on the scheme at least a partial principle of selectivity: twenty writers try to tell us what is going on of importance in Europe, which is certainly an improvement on Professor Austin's one-man band. Everything depends, of course, on the perceptiveness of the individual critic and, it must be added, the quality of the music which, in some cases, his fellow musicians are producing around him. If you have the misfortune to be a native of . . . (and every reader can fill in the blank with the country of his choice), then the commission to supply an essay of the appropriate character for an anthology of this kind must have been an unenviable one. It often happens, moreover, that the duller the country (musically speaking), the longer the essay and the more ardent the propaganda. Not all the contributions escape these faults, not even some which are written by outside authorities, for example, Mr. Nicolas Slonimsky's account of modern composition in Rumania, experienced scrutineer though he is. Paragraph after paragraph unfolds but precious little is unveiled: 'Mihail Jora commands respect as composer of fine *Lieder*. . . . One of the most enlightened composers of the Rumanian modern school is Zeno Vancea . . . Sigismund Toduta is one of the most eloquent symphonists of Rumania . . . The music of Tudor Ciortea adheres to the French tradition . . . Paul Constantinescu (1909–1963) was a Romantic Classicist . . .' And so on, and so on. One might as well study a train timetable and hope to gain therefrom a clear picture of the landscapes that will accompany one's journeys.

There are better things, of course; at least one essay, Arthur Custer's on contemporary music in Spain, suggests that it is high time that we explored seriously some of the composers he discusses, and for those who are seeking explanation or theoretical justification of the New music—a body of literature which is now greatly increasing in quantity if not in intelligibility—there is something to be gleaned from those essays which deal with the countries which have thrown up leading members of the *avant-garde*. On these grounds, indeed, it is much to be regretted that the volume's terms of reference exclude the country of origin—the United States—which has proved to be so fertile a source of many of the new movements in the arts, by no means music alone. The most striking contribution, however, is the one essay which does not investigate a geographically determined set of composers but takes up points of contrasting principle manifest in music by Boulez and Xenakis. This is Daniel Charles's 'Entr'acte: "Formal" or "Informal" Music?', an elaborate, intelligent and challenging examination of the philosophy of two exponents of the New. It is a piquant fact that so much of the writing about the New music is just as difficult and intractable as the music itself; nonetheless, it is worth persevering with this formidable piece, which, by selecting two figures of importance and focusing a strong and concentrated beam of light on them, generally illuminates the contemporary musical scene in a manner beyond the reach of Austinesque comprehensiveness.

Those who recall the so very recent days when Boulez was hailed as the dominant member of the postwar *avant-garde* may be amused to find that, in Mr. Charles's view, his 'loyalty to the Western heritage'—'his irrepressible penchant for craftsmanship, for the finely wrought work, for the severity of the finished product'—makes him a suspect figure, an exponent of 'formalism'. (It is ironical indeed that this term, so beloved of commentators in the Soviet Union, should achieve fresh currency in so unlikely a context.) Boulez, Mr. Charles suggests by his approving use of the following quotation from Heinz-Klaus Metzger, may have seemed to have been burying tradition, but in fact the funeral celebrations only established the traditional affiliations of some of the chief mourners:

The great conceptions of Boulez, Stockhausen and Pousseur draw their strength not only from their quasi-systematic consistency, but equally from the way they 'compose out' their historical positional value, and as their act of negation emphasizes the concept of what is negated, this concept gives them an exclusive claim to be the legitimate tradition.

So Boulez, in saying No, was really saying Yes, which is doubtless the reason why so many musicians, puzzled though they might be by his works, found them to be more like music than 'music'. Xenakis, on the other hand, began with 'a radical re-examination of the whole of Western tradition', and we probably don't do him an injustice if we think of his aim as 'music' rather than music. Mr. Charles's higher theoretical flights are not always easy to follow, but whereas Boulez's *'estheticism limits his view of history to the mere* (sic) *history of music'*, Xenakis takes as his point of departure *'the history of civilization as such'* (author's italics). It is scarcely possible in a short space to give Mr. Charles's account of Xenakis's mode of operation the consideration it warrants. Indeed, if the composer takes the 'history of civilization' as potential material for his music—and the laws of probability and modern physics, it seems, are all grist to his mill—then the attempt to comprehend his references and his method could be time and space consuming. In any event on this occasion it is obligatory to skip the steps in Mr. Charles's disquisition and jump to his conclusion, which would seem to have a bearing on the central feature of so much of the New music by which we are confronted. In short, away with the formalistic aesthetic which stresses 'the autonomy of the work of art and harks back to the Hegelian idea of the primacy of an "artificial" over a "natural" Beautiful' and on with the 'informal' aesthetic, 'which amounts to a blurring of the classical oppositions between art and nature, art and technique'.

This 'blurring' is indeed one of the characteristics of the New music which is most powerfully anti-traditional in intent and effect (it is not to be confused with good old-fashioned Impressionism, of course) and which arouses feelings of the intensest bewilderment in the uninitiated. Crudely stated—and one is aware of the painful oversimplification—it is a situation in which the listener finds himself unable to distinguish between sound and noise; and the moment this happens, which these days is not infrequent, the audience is adrift on a sea without compass or charts. Boulez, as Mr. Charles himself obligingly tells us, has defined the distinction between sound and noise in terms of 'the possibility and the impossibility of perceiving a structuration'. Mr. Charles cites this intelligent observation only to refute it, as part of Boulez's dependence on an 'evolutionary mode of thinking'. But whatever arguments Mr. Charles may muster, most thoughtful musicians (and listeners) will agree that it is just the amorphousness and vagueness of much of the newest music, and the consequent impossibility of discerning a perceptible structuration, that leave even the most open ears thoroughly baffled.

For all the ardour of the wholesale abolitionists of tradition, the New music too, perhaps comfortingly, has a past. The flourishing and sometimes entertaining disciples of John Cage, for example, often revive memories of the carefree days of Surrealism and Dada; and Expressionism also has had a fresh lease of life (it is one of the curiosities of the present musical scene that many a new composition trails along in the wake of the visual arts). Even the postwar pioneers in the electronic field have a venerable fatherfigure in the shape of Edgard Varèse, whose music already in the 1920s and 1930s aspired to the electronic condition, long in advance of the equipment that made electronic music finally possible. Fernand Ouellette's study of the composer[1] is only the first step towards the documentation of a gritty, uncompromising artist—'there is nobility in his noise', says Stravinsky—but it contains much valuable biographical and bibliographical matter. There are no

---

[1] *Edgard Varèse*, Paris, 1966.

music examples, alas, and the commentary on the works rarely rises above the level of enthusiastic description.

Altogether more important as a document is Pierre Schaeffer's voluminous *Traité des objets musicaux*, a massive volume of nearly 700 pages, which is further supplemented by three gramophone records and a detailed text-book in three languages (a French-English-German script which helpfully parallels the spoken word on the disc and identifies the music—or 'music'—examples).[1] M. Schaeffer, of course, is one of the best-known of those postwar pioneers mentioned above: indeed, a useful chronological list in Professor Austin's compendium isolates 1948 as a date of some significance, the year in which M. Schaeffer inaugurated his conception of *musique concrète* in a studio of the French Radio. M. Schaeffer's elaborate and exhaustive treatise is certainly authoritative and, together with the discs, forms a kind of superior do-it-yourself electronic kit—all that is missing is the equipment. There can be no doubt that M. Schaeffer has won for himself a place in the history of music, the more so now when the distinction between the two electronic schools, between the advocates of concrete sounds and 'pure' sounds electronically generated, has virtually disappeared and both schools would seem to pursue a common electronic aim. M. Schaeffer, whose intelligence and integrity are beyond question, sets out three problems for our consideration: 'the first relates to the correlation between sound . . . and the sum of the psychological phenomena of perception which constitute the sound object'; 'the second relates to the choice of definite objects which are deemed suitable for music by reason of their perceptive criteria, and leads to a sound morphology and a musical typology' (M. Schaeffer has much to say about morphology and typology in his treatise); and finally there is a third problem, 'that of the value that such objects take on within a

---

[1] Paris, 1966, 1967.

musical composition or, reciprocally, of the nature of the music (or musics) which the choice of certain musical objects implies'.

M. Schaeffer is an honest thinker and confesses freely that how we hear his 'objects' is by no means a simple question. 'Each one of us,' he writes, 'hears with different ears: sometimes too refined, sometimes too coarse, but in any event always "informed" by all kinds of prejudices and preconditioned by education.' And again: 'Sound still remains to be deciphered, whence the idea of a sol-fa of the sound object to train the ear to listen in a new way; this requires that the conventional listening habits imparted by education first be unlearned' (it should be explained perhaps that M. Schaeffer's anthology of discs is entitled *Solfège de l'objet sonore*).

So we must learn to unlearn, to become, somehow, the *first* listener! There's the rub; and one fears that most preconditioned ears, however sympathetically inclined, will find M. Schaeffer's 'objects' either more noise than sound, because they are so primitively non-musical and concretely like themselves—an example is M. Schaeffer's own *Variations for a Door and a Sigh*—or more like orthodox music, in which case associations and references are set up which always seem to work to the electronic composer's disadvantage (the sound, one feels, would have been ten times more interesting if handled by a composer manipulating a conventional medium). As it often happens that we are confronted by a mixture of components, of 'objects', small wonder that confusion, and eventually irritation and boredom, overtake the listener. Once again it is that 'blurring' which sticks in our ears, if not in our throats. M. Schaeffer seems to echo Mr. Daniel Charles's words on the reduction of the classical oppositions between art and nature when he suggests that 'Music is . . . ever groping its way . . . between nature and culture.' This may be so in our time, but in view of the chaos and incomprehension that have been the consequences of this philosophy, one wonders if the moment is not near when we ought to grope our way back and re-assert those valuable oppositions. Might it not be that our contemporary composers are pursuing an illusion?

The blurring of the distinction between sound and noise is sufficient alone to mark off the New music from the modern movement of the 1920s and 1930s. So radical a change of direction in the composer's approach to his materials (not to speak of the radically altered materials themselves) means that, for once, new is indeed New, and that it would be unrealistic to sit back and wait for the unfolding of time to reveal Xenakis or Schaeffer or Stockhausen (or whoever it may be) as the Schoenberg, Berg or Bartók of the second half of the twentieth century. But of course it is not only the conception of sound, and the raw material of sound, that has undergone a dramatic sea-change. Form too, inevitably, has been drastically revised (and become largely inaudible in the process). If further evidence were required of the yawning gulf that divides the old master from the new, one only needs to glance at two recent manuals on form, both of them from Germany. Herr Stockmeier's neat little book, *Musikalische Formprinzipien*,[1] encompasses the classical procedures of organization and it is with an almost poignant feeling that one discovers how comfortably and with what justice the once wrangled-over and hotly disputed figures of Schoenberg, Stravinsky, Bartók, Berg, *et al.*, fit into this ordered context. There they are, snugly at home in the *classical* tradition to which they belong. We can put our banners away.

A very different picture is presented by Herr Boehmer's book *Zur Theorie der offenen Form in der Neuen Musik*,[2] in which there is certainly no room for the *ancien régime* in chapters devoted to the 'open' forms of the New music: the aleatoric, the indeterminate, structural variability,

---

[1] Cologne, 1967.   [2] Darmstadt, 1967.

structural mobility, and so forth. One has to grasp a new terminology and a new notation—indeed, a comparison of the music examples from both books is a short way of coming to realize how remote the past could seem to ears and minds attuned to Herr Boehmer's way of thinking. He is a composer himself and writes with confidence and not always uncritically about 'Chance as Ideology', 'Expectation and Probability', and other related topics; but the awful suspicion persists, even as one perseveres, that though one may master his analyses, experience of the music will still defeat one. Never, one begins to feel, has such a torrent of words been released in the cause of comprehension; and yet never have the forms of music—the objects of the verbal exercise—remained so obstinately inaccessible.

Herr Stockmeier's manual, appropriately enough in the chapter on 'The Motive', includes one quotation from Webern (there is some significance in the fact that one would find it less easy to quote from Webern in the succeeding chapter on 'The Theme'). No one would deny that it is certainly possible to see Webern too as part of the great tradition. After all, so many of the virtues of his music—its precision, clarity, formal perfection, etc.—represent qualities that we admire daily in classical composers. Moreover, the virtues of Webern appear all the more marked in view of the development of the history of music post-Webern. We have to remember, nonetheless, that the term 'post-Webern' at one time usefully fitted a whole school of composers, active after the Second World War, when it seemed possible that it was through the discovery of Webern's art that music might renew itself. The activity was widespread, influential, but comparatively short-lived. Webern, naturally enough, does not have much of a role to play in Herr Boehmer's study. Do we, then, relegate Webern to tradition? Or was he responsible for more than a renewal—in fact, for the creation of the New?

None of the present run of studies of Webern tackles these central questions, and least of all Friedrich Wildgan's slender book,[1] the biographical part of which reads quite charmingly if one is prepared to accept a tone of voice which is distinctly parochial (Herr Wildgans might well be writing about Professor Austin's Joseph Haas). The 'Critical Catalogue of Works' is a pitiful affair, void of meaningful music examples, and conveying less information than one expects nowadays to buy with one's concert programme.

The inadequacy of this effort points up the need for a full-scale examination of Webern's work, which will not only 'place' him in relation to tradition but also investigate the extent and meaning of his postwar influence.[2] Such a study must constitute a skilful exercise in the art of perspective; but once again it is perspective that is required to illuminate both Webern's particular contribution and our general condition: or should it be plight?

No one in his senses could blame this most fastidious of composers for many of the anxieties that assail us. No musician, surely, was more conscious of the distinction between sound and noise, and there have been few composers prepared to leave so little to chance, which could never have been an ideology for Webern. Nor can he be held responsible for our expanding electronic universe. Nonetheless, the radical shift in his art towards abstraction, which was, of course, bound up with the nature of his technique, opened up paths for the future of the gravest consequence. It was a mode of thinking which, if it did not actually create the New, instead created certain new possibilities, among them—dare one say it?—that dehumanization of the art of music which is perhaps today's bleakest prospect. It is a disconcerting fact that, wide though the contemporary composer's search is for creative stimulus—

---

[1] *Anton Webern*, London, 1966.

[2] This need has since been met, to a degree at least, by Walter Kolneder's book, *Anton Webern: An Introduction to His Works*, London and Berkeley, 1968.

we may remind ourselves that Xenakis's is no less than the 'history of civilization'—an audience, not to speak of performers, rarely receives consideration, even in passing. One doubts if 'music' will be able to drop its inverted commas until that essential and humane relationship between composer and public, between the composer and the user of his music, has been restored.

INDEX

Index

Index

Index

Index

Index

[The Index compiled by Terence A. Miller,
Member of the Society of Indexers.]